Inside Beethoven's Quartets

Inside Beethoven's Quartets

History, Interpretation, Performance

Lewis Lockwood

and

The Juilliard String Quartet

Joel Smirnoff, Ronald Copes, Samuel Rhodes, Joel Krosnick

Harvard University Press

Cambridge, Massachusetts ◇ London, England ◇ 2008

Publication of this book has been supported through the generous provisions of the Maurice and Lula Bradley Smith Memorial Fund

The score of the first version of opus 18 no. 1 is reproduced by permission of the publishers from *Beethoven Werke*, Abteilung VI, Band 3, *Streichquartette I,* copyright © 1996 G. Henle Verlag, Munich

Library of Congress Cataloging-in-Publication Data

Lockwood, Lewis.
Inside Beethoven's quartets : history, interpretation, performance /
Lewis Lockwood and the Juilliard String Quartet,
Joel Smirnoff, Ronald Copes, Samuel Rhodes, Joel Krosnick.
   p.   cm.
Includes bibliographical references (p.   ) and index.
ISBN-13: 978-0-674-02809-8 (cloth : alk. paper)
1. Beethoven, Ludwig van, 1770–1827. Quartets, strings.
2. String quartets—Analysis, appreciation.
I. Juilliard String Quartet.   II. Title.
ML410.B42L63 2008
785'.7194092—dc22   2007043106

CONTENTS

∞

AUDIO CD

Op. 18 no. 1, mvt. 1 (final version)

Op. 18 no. 1, mvt. 1 (Amenda version)

Op. 59 no. 1, mvt. 1

Op. 130, mvt. 1

PREFACE

> A description of [the city of] Zaira as it is today should contain all
> Zaira's past. The city, however, does not tell its past, but contains it
> like the lines of a hand, written in the corners of the streets, the grat-
> ings of the windows, the banisters of the steps, the antennae of the
> lightning rods, the poles of the flags, every segment marked in turn
> with scratches, indentations, scrolls.
>
> Italo Calvino, *Invisible Cities*

Following Calvino, I imagine the world of classical music in our time
as an invisible city whose present contains its past—a past inscribed on
it "like the lines of a hand" that, as the image suggests, imply its history and foretell its future. My imagined inhabitants are musical citi-
zens of many kinds: performers of vocal and instrumental music, composers, scholars, critics, teachers, students, concertgoers, music lovers,
and casual listeners. Many have more than one strong interest and en-
joy more than one kind of music. Two groups among them, the performers and the scholars, typically live in different neighborhoods,

teach in different kinds of schools, mostly address different publics, and rarely communicate with each other.

The performers spend their days engaged in playing or singing, rehearsing, preparing concerts, perfecting their techniques, developing their interpretations, making recordings, teaching their students, living the active lives of professional music-makers. Their habitats are practice rooms, studios, and concert halls. The performers know that most of the compositions of past eras that they play every day have complex histories and origins, but they rarely have time to pursue historical or critical issues behind the works. Their job is to bring music to life in performance and to interpret it well. They are deeply engaged in the practical tasks of preparing performances down to the last detail.

The scholars spend their days thinking, reading, listening, writing essays or books, teaching classes or seminars, preparing lectures, studying in libraries or in their private studies, living the contemplative lives of historians or critics. A few scholars work regularly with performers and many are themselves skilled amateur performers who understand the art and craft of music-making. In fact many members of the two groups know more about each other and their domains than might generally be supposed, though their paths rarely cross in public.

Still, if the history of this invisible city is indeed inscribed upon it, that history can be discovered in its concert halls, its schools of music, its practice rooms, its university and high-school classrooms, its music libraries, and its lecture halls. It is imprinted on the memories, imaginations, hearts, voices, and hands of all as denizens of one city.

This book attempts to link musical scholarship and performance. For me its origins go back to 1990. I had taught music history at Princeton and then at Harvard, and had studied Beethoven, his music and his life, for many years. In the fall of 1989 there came an invitation, out of the blue, from the Juilliard School of Music to give a set of public lectures on the Beethoven Quartets together with the Juilliard String Quartet. The Quartet was then still led by its founding first violinist, Robert Mann, one of the outstanding quartet leaders of the twentieth century, and its other members were Joel Smirnoff as second violin, Samuel Rhodes, viola, and Joel Krosnick, cello.

In my first cordial meeting with the Quartet members we made plans for three public sessions of two hours each, dealing with one Beethoven quartet at each session–one early, one middle-period, one late. I suggested we focus on op. 18 no. 1, op. 59 no. 1, and op. 130 (with its two finales, the Grosse Fuge and the second, "little" finale that Beethoven wrote to replace the fugue when he published it as a separate piece). I hoped that the Juilliard members would not only play examples, as they were glad to do, but join actively in the discussions, contribute their ideas about the works, and make the lectures as interactive as possible. They needed no urging. In the first session, on early Beethoven, after I set the stage with some remarks on Haydn and Mozart as Beethoven's major predecessors, I introduced op. 18 no. 1 and briefly compared the two surviving versions of the work (a complete preliminary version has come down to us, by chance) with the audience following printed scores. The Juilliard Quartet members commented on the two versions and played the entire early version.

In the first lecture I did most of the talking, though all four Quartet members contributed remarks as well. By the second lecture, on the "Razumovsky" Quartets, they were talking a lot more, and by the third lecture, the organizers had to set up four microphones for them on the stage, which they put to heavy use for comments on many aspects of op. 130. Hearing these experienced professional performers not only play but share their ideas on performance and analysis, on music and musical life, interacting with me and with the audience, was a pleasure for everyone. Ideas flowed back and forth among us on the compositional backgrounds of these Beethoven quartets, on their place in the history of the genre, on the inner character of the musical material of each movement and the Quartet's ideas on how to create a performance that would shape and reflect the tonal architecture of a Beethoven quartet in the concert hall. Working together at these intensive sessions, the Quartet and I converted what might have been just a lecture with some musical illustrations into a relaxed and collegial joint seminar. The audience participated with questions and comments as well.

Thirteen years later, in May 2003, I was again asked to join the Juilliard Quartet for an evening presentation at the Library of Congress, where they were playing a Beethoven cycle on the famous matched Stradivarius instruments kept in the Whittall Pavilion. This time we delivered a joint discussion of Beethoven's op. 95 and op. 127 for a large audience. By now Robert Mann had retired; Joel Smirnoff had become the new first violinist, and Ronald Copes was the new second violinist. And from this second collaboration, in 2003, but with memories of the 1990 lectures in the background, we jointly developed the idea of a book on selected Beethoven quartets that could embody our respective contributions, mine through historical and analytical material and theirs through their performances on CD made for this book and through annotated scores of the three quartets to be discussed. We also planned to include joint commentary on all three works. From the beginning the idea was that the book would contain scores of the movements to be discussed and annotated by the Juilliard Quartet–inevitably not the entire works, for reasons of space limitations. As before we chose op. 18 no. 1 (with its two versions), op. 59 no. 1, and op. 130.

My own contributions to this book are offered in three chapters, each in two parts. The first part introduces each work and places it in historical context; the second part focuses on what we know of the compositional background of the first movement through its surviving sketches or Beethoven's autograph manuscript, depending on the availability of these sources. This kind of evidence survives in different ways for the three works. For the op. 18 quartets we have ample sketches but no autographs, while for op. 59 no. 1 it is just the opposite: we have a richly informative autograph manuscript but few sketches. For op. 130 we have both, although no exhaustive study of the first-movement sketches has yet been published.

The Juilliard Quartet's contributions are offered in the annotated scores, the conversations about the works (in which I joined them), and the accompanying CD which they recorded especially for this book. For the annotated scores they have devised comments and symbols that represent their collective thinking about myriad details of performance—dynamics, nuances of tempo, articulation, qualities of sound—all the elements that go into their meticulously prepared performances of these and other works. And in the conversations their rich experience as ensemble performers and teachers emerges in vivid detail about many issues and problems that come up in the three quite different movements, and in ways that invite further thought and discussion.

To sum up, the main idea of the book is to provide a record of professional interaction and exchange of ideas on current scholarship and performance, with Beethoven at the center. We hope the book will be read and used by performers, by scholars and students, and above all by general readers and music-lovers who care about chamber music and about the Beethoven quartets. Inevitably some parts of the discussion will be of greater interest to the general reader than others, but with the scores and recordings included, nothing in the book should be inaccessible to anyone who has a modicum of musical background and an interest in the subject.

No single book can do more than sample the varied categories of experience and knowledge that are possessed by music historians on the one hand and by performers on the other. But we hope this book may show how collaborative interaction can help to integrate forms of experience that too often stand far apart, and may stimulate further ventures of this kind.

Lewis Lockwood
Brookline, Massachusetts, 2007

NOTE ON THE SCORES

The annotated scores in this volume are based on the standard collected edition, *Beethovens Werke: Vollständige kritische durchgesehene Gesamtaugabe,* 25 vols. (Leipzig: Breitkopf und Härtel, 1862–1865). Annotations are indicated by italics (for dynamic indications and other words and phrases); dotted lines (for slurs and crescendo/decrescendo marks); and smaller size (for articulation marks on individual notes). All up-bow and down-bow markings, as well as fingerings, are annotations. In addition the following special symbols are used:

Comma	Short breath or separation between phrases, not necessarily a break
Comma with slash	Very small amount of extra time, to set off a subito piano
Right arrow	Moving ahead or recovery of tempo
Left arrow	Slowing down or hesitation
Wavy line	Rubato, usually taking time to highlight an event in the music
Brackets	Used to clarify phrasing or indicate principal voice

Opus 18 no. 1

THE OPUS 18 QUARTETS

"THAT NOBLE GENRE"

In 1832, five years after Beethoven's death, Ignaz von Seyfried completed a biographical memoir that mingled recollections, anecdotes, and musical opinions. Seyfried, a seasoned Viennese musician, had known Beethoven for about thirty years and had conducted many of his orchestral works as well as his opera *Leonore* in 1805 and 1806. Since Seyfried was an active composer and conductor but not a string player, what he has to say about Beethoven's string quartets reflects the strong response that these works aroused generally among contemporary musicians. After a lengthy description of Beethoven's keyboard duel with the pianist Joseph Wölffl, in 1799, Seyfried turns to Beethoven as quartet composer around 1806, when he was writing the three op. 59 works:

> In this period Beethoven sought to bring about profound achievements in quartet style—that noble genre, which had

been reformed by Haydn, or, better, conjured up by him out of nothing, and which Mozart's universal genius had enriched with still deeper content and luxuriantly blooming fantasy. Now finally our Beethoven took those culminating steps that could only be attempted by one who was predestined to do so, and in which he could hardly be followed by anyone else.

There now developed his close and friendly relations with the chamber music virtuosi of Count Razumovsky— Schuppanzigh, Weiss, and Linke, to whom he then entrusted his entire [quartet] output, and he communicated to them his ideas on performance and expression and on the spirit of these works. And so it was that in Vienna people were heard to say, "Whoever wants to really understand and appreciate Beethoven's works for stringed instruments really well, must hear them performed by these master artists." At least that is the competent opinion of those who are really informed about these matters . . . Now also [in 1832] the first two leaves of this wonderful trifolium have fallen.[1]

Seyfried's dates are not quite right, as Beethoven had known the violinist Ignaz Schuppanzigh and the violist Franz Weiss since the 1790s, but his spirit of admiration is convincing. This passage reflects the central role of Beethoven's early and middle-period quartets in the European chamber music culture of the 1830s, a position they held throughout the nineteenth century and continue to hold despite the momentous transformations of musical style and musical life since then. For Seyfried the quartet was essentially for knowledgeable enthusiasts, not for the broad general public, even though quartet recitals were becoming more frequent. Even now some consider it an art form primarily for connoisseurs and one that continues to reflect its past glories, despite so many significant contributions by later composers.

As Seyfried implies, in Beethoven's lifetime the quartets of Haydn and Mozart were living classics, something like Old and New Testaments of chamber music. They loomed large not only as models for Beethoven but as staples of the everyday repertoire, along with works by lesser contemporaries. As Beethoven first challenged the quartet canon in the 1790s and then dramatically enlarged its expressive range in his middle-period quartets, Haydn and Mozart remained a significant presence for him, and he directly emulated them in some of his works.[2] Though Seyfried does not mention Beethoven's late quartets, completed between 1824 and 1826 and still new and strange when Seyfried was writing in the early 1830s, he probably saw that despite their seeming obscurity they were a summa of Beethoven's lifetime achievement.

Seyfried pays personal tribute to Beethoven's favorite players: the violinist Ignaz Schuppanzigh (jocularly known as Falstaff or "Mylord" in Beethoven's circle), the violist Franz Weiss, and the cellist Joseph Linke. All were members of the quartet maintained until about 1815 by Count Andreas Razumovsky, for some years Russian ambassador to the Austrian court and for whom Beethoven wrote the three quartets of op. 59, and they remained close to the composer for many years. Seyfried may have known them as prominent first-desk players in some of his orchestral performances, but his special mention of them as a "trifolium" speaks to the quality of their work in chamber music. Reflecting that nostalgic devotion to the memory of earlier performances that has always marked chamber music lovers, Seyfried laments that their fine playing would not be matched in later times. Important too is his suggestion that the intimate, personal character of the Beethoven quartets emerges not only from the works themselves, as abstract entities, but from their interpretation by the ripest and best performers.

That implication also informs this book, in which historical and critical thinking about the Beethoven quartets is joined by commentary and insights on performance provided by the Juilliard String Quartet, one of the leading ensembles of our time. Our aim is to establish a balance between analytical-historical knowledge and the direct experience of performers.

∞

Beethoven came late to quartet writing. Since his arrival from provincial Bonn in 1792, he had taken Vienna by storm as the most brilliant younger pianist-composer of the time and was on his way to fulfilling his patrons' prophecies that he would become "a second Mozart." By the time he started work on his first string quartets in 1799, aged twenty-eight, Beethoven was the young lion of Austrian and German musical life, and his reputation was rapidly spreading through Europe. By now he had composed his first eight piano sonatas—a quarter of his lifetime output—and many sets of piano variations, two piano concertos, the first four piano trios, two cello sonatas, and three violin sonatas, along with much other chamber music, including the highly original string trios he published as op. 9. Contemporary patrons hoped that he would inherit "the spirit of Mozart from the hands of Haydn," as his friend Count Waldstein had expressed it in 1792, in the wake of Mozart's death in 1791. By 1799 Beethoven was rising to the challenge: he was working on his first symphony and had his first quartets under way, thus competing with Haydn in the two genres in which Haydn had been the prime mover and in which Haydn and Mozart had been the dominating masters.

It was in this spirit that, in 1800, Prince Karl Lichnowsky pinned his faith on Beethoven and the future of the genre by making him a generous gift of two violins, a viola, and a cello, hoping to spur him to write new quartets. That Beethoven prized the instruments is clear from his reference to them in his Heiligenstadt Testament of 1802.[3] Lichnowsky's gesture may have been suggested by his house violinist, Ignaz Schuppanzigh, when Beethoven was composing and revising his first quartets, the six of op. 18. From 1794 to 1799 Lichnowsky sponsored a regular quartet ensemble led by the young Schuppanzigh, with Franz Weiss as violist and as cellist either Anton Kraft or his son, Nikolaus.[4] Beethoven had grown up at Bonn with first-class string players, among them Andreas Romberg, Joseph Reicha, and Bernhard Romberg; and at Bonn he had also taken some lessons on the violin and viola. In Vienna his close circle included Schuppanzigh and the violinists Wenzel Krumpholz and Franz Clement. But the chamber music circle around Lichnowsky was the nesting-ground for his growing knowledge of the quartet literature. As Anton Schindler put it, years later, "It was in this company of performing artists that Beethoven learned what he needed to know about the playing of stringed instruments."[5]

The string quartet had emerged in the second half of the century as the central vehicle for serious chamber music and as a new field for master and journeyman composers alike. Arising alongside the four-movement symphony, it shared a founding father in the "inexhaustible" Haydn, as Waldstein called him, who had begun as early as the 1760s to explore the new range of tone colors and sonorities that emerged when four solo strings played as an independent ensemble, freed from dependence on the harpsichord and other continuo instruments that had long been essential in Baroque style. With their partly overlapping ranges, the instruments of the quartet offered the full array of registers needed for tonal composition while providing the completely unified sound-palette that could otherwise be found only in music for winds or solo keyboard. Above all, as Haydn had brilliantly shown from the 1760s on, the quartet offered an aesthetic arena for the four most agile and versatile of instruments, instruments that could blend perfectly with one another, shift their modes of expression with quicksilver flexibility, and engage in complex dialogues in a wide range of musical contexts.

Although there were alternative ensemble combinations, the string quartet rose to a privileged position. It challenged young composers to prove their competence by writing in a range of "pure" styles that this ensemble seemed to favor, styles that flowed naturally out of the intimate character of quartet playing. At one extreme this could mean rigorous contrapuntal part-writing, which was mentioned by the theorist Heinrich Koch as characteristic of good quartet composition.[6] Fugal writing appears more readily in the quartets of Haydn, Mozart, and Beethoven than in their other chamber music—witness the fugal finales of Haydn's op. 20 quartets, the finale of Mozart's first mature quartet, K. 387, the development sections of the first and last movements of Beethoven's op. 18 no. 1, and the finale of op. 59 no. 3. But while the quartet lent itself to textures in which the first violin was the clear leading voice accompanied by the lower three, it also accommodated other types of dialogue and motivic interplay in which any of the four instruments could be the temporary leader. These textures were first revealed in Haydn's early and middle-period quartets, further developed by Mozart in the 1780s, expanded still further in Haydn's late quartets of the 1790s, and then dramatically developed by Beethoven.

While Beethoven was gaining a foothold in Vienna, Haydn was at the crest of his career, consolidating his European eminence. As productive as ever, he wrote his twelve "London" symphonies for his journeys to England in 1791–92 and 1794–95, and he further enhanced his legacy with other vocal and instrumental works, perhaps most significantly with a raft of new quartets. Raising his achievements in this genre to even greater heights than before, he composed his last twenty quartets, grouped as op. 64 (1790), opp. 71 and 74 (1793), op. 76 (1797), and, finally, the two of op. 77 (1799).

Alongside Haydn, but before Haydn's last period, Mozart had once again turned to the genre with the six quartets that he dedicated to Haydn and published in 1785. Far more developed than Mozart's earlier quartets, these works combined imagination and depth of expression that matched Haydn's best and set an even higher standard for rival composers. Though Beethoven knew and admired Haydn, and learned much from him, Mozart's quartets were significant models for him from the beginning to the end of his career—and not just for his quartets. We know this from Beethoven's comments as reported by contemporaries, but even more from the works themselves. Clear witnesses are those compositions that feature mysterious slow introductions with unstable harmonies, which are broadly or directly conceived in the image of the great opening Adagio of Mozart's "Dissonant" quartet, K. 465.[7] After the pinnacle of 1785, Mozart followed with the single "Hoffmeister" Quartet, K. 499 (1786) and the three "Prussian" Quartets, K. 575, 589, and 590, of 1789 and 1790, plus his masterly string quintets and the string trio in E-flat, K. 563.

That Haydn's last quartets were all written after 1785, the majority after Mozart's death in December 1791, suggests that he too may have refashioned some aspects of his quartet writing in view of the new heights Mozart had reached. The death of Mozart may possibly have helped clear some of the new imaginative space that Haydn needed for his remarkable productivity of the 1790s. Although common opinion sees Haydn as Mozart's ancestor, the fact remains that Mozart's six quartets of 1785 predated most of the later Haydn quartets and may have exerted as strong an influence on them as Haydn's earlier masterpieces had done on Mozart's quartets; their complex relationship is still poorly understood. The young Beethoven, coming of age in Bonn and then in Vienna after 1792, would have known Mozart's quartets as they became available, and he probably knew a great many earlier Haydn quartets as well as the late masterworks.

OTHER EARLY CHAMBER MUSIC FOR STRINGS

Beethoven had to learn how to write for strings because he was primarily a pianist who improvised and composed at the keyboard. During his first five years in Vienna he worked hard at both performing and composing. Although he had studied violin as well as piano in his apprentice years and had played viola in the Bonn orchestra, he experimented only slowly and gradually with music for string ensembles. In 1793–1794 he fashioned a string quintet by revising a wind octet he had written in Bonn in 1792, and he liked it well enough to bring it out in 1796 as his op. 4.[8] His first three piano trios (op. 1) showed solid understanding of violin technique and of the newly expanding capacities of the cello, which he then elaborated in his two cello sonatas, op. 5. Comparable exploration of idiomatic string writing appears in his earliest violin sonatas, beginning with a few experimental works and culminating in the trilogy of op. 12 (1797–1798), which contemporary critics found unusually difficult.[9]

In his first Vienna years he wrote as many as six string trios before trying even a single quartet. The first was a Bonn divertimento that he revised and published as op. 3. Then came two Serenades, op. 8 and op. 25, lighter works that nevertheless contained some serious movements. But in 1797–1798 he deepened his art with the three string trios of op. 9, proudly claiming in the dedication that "the author will have the satisfaction of presenting to the first patron of his Muse the best of his works."[10] All three, especially the C minor, no. 3, show his command of a difficult medium. The string trio had to encompass the same four-part tonal harmonic progressions and varied types of thematic and motivic dialogue that appeared in the string quartet but were much harder to achieve with three string parts. Only Mozart, with his usual mastery, had left an absolute model, his E-flat Divertimento K. 563, of 1788.

In the fall of 1798 Beethoven accepted Prince Lobkowitz's commission for a set of six quartets. He immersed himself in the modern classics of the genre, many of which he had probably played and heard in Bonn. He had laboriously copied movements from Haydn's op. 20 and from Mozart's 1785 quartets, and was not above performing and studying quartets by at least a few local masters, including Emanuel Förster. In his memoir of Beethoven, Franz Wegeler reports in this connection that "a Viennese composer, Förster, brought him a quartet [presumably a string quartet] that he had just finished copying out that morning. In the development section of the first movement the cellist lost his place. Beethoven stood up and sang the cello part, while continuing to play his own part. When I told him that this was a mark of his remarkable skill, he replied, 'that's the way the bass part had to go, unless the composer had known nothing about composition.'"[11] Mastering the medium in his own strongly profiled musical language took hard work, as we see from his sketches and from the full-scale revision of op. 18 no. 1 that is discussed in detail below.

Lobkowitz's request inevitably quickened Beethoven's rivalry with Haydn, who accepted a commission from the same patron at the same time. The outcome showed where the two composers stood. Haydn was then busy with his two major oratorios, *The Creation* and *The Seasons*, and he finished only two of the expected six of his op. 77.[12] For Beethoven, though, creating six matched quartets was a major challenge. Accordingly, he revised the op. 18 quartets heavily and at least two, perhaps all six, passed through more than one complete version. Most of the evidence for these revisions has to be gleaned from sketches or early copied parts, but for the F major quartet, op. 18 no. 1, a happy accident of history has preserved a complete early version. Beethoven sent a preliminary copy of the entire work to his close friend Karl Amenda, then later asked Amenda not to circulate it because he had revised it, "having now learned how to write string quartets properly."[13] A comparison of the two versions reveals Beethoven's growing understanding of compositional and idiomatic issues in quartet writing, and shows his self-criticism in action.[14]

His sketchbooks tell us much about the individual quartets of op. 18, but also about his idea of how to order the set of six. It's clear that Beethoven composed them in this order: no. 3 in D major; no. 1 in F major; no. 2 in G major; no. 5 in A major; and no. 6 in B-flat major. We are not sure about the origins of no. 4 in C minor because no sketches for it appear in his sketchbooks. It has been suggested that the C minor might have been an earlier work, perhaps already composed in Bonn. But for such an early dating there is no hard evidence, nor is there any solid reason to regard it as less developed than the others. I believe that Beethoven worked on the C minor quartet at the same time as the others, but probably on loose sketch pages that did not survive.

In ordering the "opus" Beethoven followed common practice. The usual plan was to begin with the longest and most elaborate of the six quartets, a role that clearly belongs to his F major quartet. That five out of six should be in major keys, one in minor, is also traditional, and, as the single minor-mode work, his robust no. 4, however different in character from its models, would have been as strong an answer as he could then make to Mozart's D minor (K. 428) and Haydn's B minor op. 33 no. 1 (1781) and F-sharp minor op. 50 no. 4 (1787). Fresh in current memory were Haydn's minor-mode quartets of the 1790s, including the G minor, op. 74 no. 3 of 1793 ("The Rider"), and the D minor "Quinten" Quartet, op. 76 no. 2 (1796). As his friends noted, Beethoven avoided D minor as the basic key for a string quartet all his life, thus keeping clear of comparison with Mozart and Haydn even in his later years, when he had moved beyond them. His later minor-mode works—the powerfully original E minor quartet op. 59 no. 2, the terse op. 95 in F minor, and the transcendental op. 132 in A minor—are in keys in which Mozart wrote no string quartets and Haydn only two, his op. 20 no. 5 and op. 55 no. 2 in F minor, which Beethoven must certainly have known well.

All this is important because of a tendency in the critical literature to relegate op. 18 to a secondary status among Beethoven's earlier works. This view is partly based on his patent emulation of Mozart in several of them, above all op. 18 no. 5 in A major (modeled broadly on Mozart's A major quartet K. 464), and less overtly, op. 18 no. 6, which bears some relationship to Mozart's "Dissonant" Quartet. But his reliance on Mozart was no weakness. The signal aesthetic problem he faced in these years was how to find his own strong compositional voice when he had grown up steeped in the music of two predecessors as great as Haydn and Mozart. In op. 18 no. 5, as in other works that show Mozartian influences, he is never more himself than when he is working directly against a Mozartian template, as he sketches the larger shapes of movements and develops musical ideas that reformulate contemporary approaches to the genre.

Contemporaries saw op. 18 as progressive; as a critic wrote about the first three quartets, "they are . . . excellent works . . . [that] fully testify to his art; but they must be played frequently and very well, since they are difficult to perform and not at all in a popular style."[15] This last was a compliment, not a criticism, for there was a general understanding that composers should display the highest craftsmanship in this most intimate of genres. Beethoven did not disappoint.

The first to be finished, op. 18 no. 3 in D major, progresses from the surface smoothness of its first movement to the rocketing pace of its Presto finale, a kind of 6/8 perpetuum mobile. The sharp contrast between the placid first movement and the bounding energy of the finale is more in Haydn's vein than in Mozart's. But Mozartian thematic ideas abound in the first movement, above all in the artful shaping of the first theme itself, with its upward leap of a seventh and then gradual descent, and in its continuation (ex. 1). The passage at mm. 17–21, at which the first violin alone, as leading voice, moves down through two octaves in undulating figures, is virtually stolen from a passage in the finale of Mozart's A major quartet K. 464, in which the first violin breaks loose in a very similar manner (ex. 2).[16]

By opening the set with the longer and more elaborate F major work, not the D major, Beethoven shows that he wanted to stake his claim with a work of decisive originality rather than with one that, however beautiful, might not carry the same weight. That he turned to the F major directly after the D major in his sketchbook suggests that this rearrangement occurred to him at an early stage, but we

Ex. 1. Beethoven, op. 18 no. 3, first movement, mm. 1–22.

also see that the Amenda version of the F major carries the heading "Quartetto Nro. II."

Yet the evidence is not entirely clear on this point. For, while composing the F major, Beethoven worked out the basic material of all its movements in sketch form and also wrote down a private remark about the next work he intended in the series. He writes, in French, that he will compose "le seconde qu[atuor] dans une style bien legère excepté le dernier pièce" (the second quartet in a lighter style, except for its finale).[17] This entry shows him composing one work while thinking about the next and about the ordering of the series. And if the G major quartet was now "le seconde," then the F major would now be the first—though he may have vacillated about this decision for a while. The entry makes a distinction between heavier and lighter "style," and thus shows him thinking about the aesthetic weight of each work as a matter of conscious choice.

Number 2 in G major is indeed lighter in tone and substance than no. 1, and is positioned as its counterweight, with the smooth D major, no. 3, in third position. The G major quartet abounds with lightness and grace, while its initial theme avoids the characteristic symmetry of many a Mozartian opening. From here on the G major deepens its expressive content. The slow movement, in two tempi and meters (an Adagio cantabile in 3/4 alternating with Allegro episodes in 2/4), has room for flights of rapid passagework for the first violin more elaborate than anywhere else in Beethoven's early ensemble writing. The Scherzo and last movement are lively and energetic. The spirit of Haydn presides over the rapid 2/4 finale, but the rebellious young Beethoven breaks out at many points, above all in the coda, where a final

Ex. 2. Mozart, Quartet in A major, K. 464, mm. 59–63.

passage brings alternating sforzando accents as the first violin and cello reduce the dynamic level from fortissimo to pianissimo in the course of twenty bars.

Quartet no. 4 moves to the dark side, where it parallels its C minor companions, the "Pathétique" piano sonata and the string trio op. 9 no. 3. The first movement unleashes emotional forces both in its C minor–E-flat major exposition and in the elaborations that follow. Its powerful registral contrasts are matched in Beethoven's Bonn works only in his Joseph Cantata. The opening theme in the first violin, with pulsating tonic repeated notes in the cello and then all three lower parts, rises with increasing power through more than two octaves. Its first eight-measure period is followed by an asymmetric five-measure continuation, reaching its first climactic fortissimo arrival at m. 13. Slashing chords in all instruments then prepare the way for the completion of the first large paragraph of the movement.

There is no true slow movement. In its place is a light, playful C major Andante scherzoso in 3/8, alternating fugato with homophonic sections and with interplay of all instruments. Its cousin is the slow movement of the First Symphony, but the quartet's Andante is more fully realized. The two movements that follow (a stormy Menuetto and an Alla breve finale) return to the C minor passion of the opening, though in the finale the many repeated subsections of the rondo create a formal squareness that makes this movement less effective than the first movement. It is a solid conclusion but does not feel like a true culmination of what has gone before.

In no. 5, in A major, a new balance emerges. Again, the general similarity to Mozart's K. 464 in the same key seems to put Beethoven in the role of imitator. Yet the two works only partly look alike, as if Beethoven were showing that he could employ a Mozartian formal plan but make it his own. The opening is utterly unlike anything in Mozart, whose themes are usually introduced fully and sequentially within a single instrumental or ensemble register. Beethoven's A major 6/8 opening "theme" arises from the interplay of two three-note motivic fragments, one in low register, one in high register, alternating between cello and first violin; the cello holds steady while the violin builds the fragments into a rising sequential theme that moves up an octave through its first ten measures. And in the opening of the finale, a parallel dialogue begins the action, now emerging from a three-note upbeat figure, with all four instruments in imitation.

With the B-flat major quartet, no. 6, we come to the richest and most conceptually advanced of these quartets. The first movement shows what can be drawn from a seemingly innocuous fourth-beat embellishment, a turning figure in sixteenth-notes. This four-note upbeat figure plus single downbeat brings dramatic results akin to those that Beethoven realizes in the first movement of his Second Symphony, which he began to sketch in late 1800 and early 1801 just as he was putting the last touches on op. 18. The slow movement of no. 6 is one of the most expressive of his early 2/4 adagio movements, and the Scherzo's manic syncopations are unparalleled in chamber music up to this time.

But if the three earlier movements are poised on the edge of experimentation, the finale goes beyond them. Its use of a programmatic title, "La Malinconia," is new to the quartet literature. We can imagine that Haydn and Mozart may have come close to implying programmatic narratives in certain expressive movements (e.g., Mozart's famous slow introduction to his C major Quartet K. 465, or Haydn's B major "Fantasia" in his op. 76 no. 6), but neither composer ever used a title of this kind. Possibly Beethoven was influenced by earlier musical depiction of the humors, or states of the soul, familiar from late Baroque and some Classical examples, and he might perhaps have known a Trio Sonata in C Minor by Carl Philipp Emanuel Bach, written in 1751, which depicts a "conversation between a sanguine person and a melancholy one."[18] We can discern just such a contrast in Beethoven's finale, in which the painfully sensitive slow introduction, with its agonizing unstable harmonies, is followed by a cheerful Allegretto in B-flat major, in 3/8, that forms the main section of the movement. At the end of the movement the melancholy introduction partly returns and enters into brief exchanges with the sanguine 3/8 thematic material, which eventually triumphs in a Prestissimo coda. The special title and tempo marking make clear that Beethoven is searching for a mode of communication about "melancholy" that explores the limits of the expressive domain of the string quartet. Below "La Malinconia" and "Adagio" he writes the special instruction, "Questo pezzo si deve trattare colla più gran delicatezza" ("This piece should be performed with the greatest possible delicacy").

This depiction of emotional states has inevitably been linked to the onset of Beethoven's deafness, which he had begun to notice in 1796 or 1797. His deafness had precipitated a severe personal crisis by 1801, as we know from his few letters about it to trusted friends—one to Amenda, the other to Wegeler—and also from the Heiligenstadt Testament, a confessional document that he wrote in the autumn of 1802, just a year after the publication of op. 18. The link is credible, even though Beethoven generally seems to have been able to cast his current miseries aside when it came to composition, finding ways to free his creative work from his physical and psychological afflictions. But the onset of deafness was devastating for a young composer-pianist forging a major public career, and we can feel that "La Malinconia" is not abstractly programmatic but is a personal reflection on extremes of emotion, in which the sanguine humor eventually overcomes the melancholy. That the most complex movement is the finale orients this last work in the set toward its ending and foreshadows the powerfully goal-directed works of his later periods.

The quartets of op. 18 are a milestone in Beethoven's development. Their wide range of aesthetic approaches equals that of the five piano sonatas that he composed between 1800 and 1801, beginning with his op. 22 in B-flat major and the A-flat Major Sonata, op. 26; the paired sonatas "quasi una fantasia," op. 27 nos. 1 and 2 (the so-called "Moonlight" sonata); and finally, the D major "Pastorale" sonata, op. 28. Taken together, op. 18 matches the piano sonata group in variety and depth, and if the quartets were not encompassed in a single opus we would probably see them in their individuality as clearly as we do the sonatas.

THE FIRST MOVEMENT

With its energy and verve the first movement stamps authority on the whole work and on the entire opus. Its combination of tempo and meter, Allegro con brio in 3/4 time, is surprisingly rare. Though Allegro con brio is a familiar tempo choice for many of Beethoven's first movements, he used it with triple meter only in his C Minor Trio, op. 1 no. 3; in the first movement of the *Eroica* Symphony; and in the Credo of his C Major Mass, op. 86.[1] Even Allegro with no modifier appears infrequently with triple meter in Beethoven's first movements, while of course it is the norm in scherzo and minuet movements.[2] The point is important because op. 18 no. 1's first movement is a rare case in which Beethoven considered both triple and duple meter, as we see from his sketches.

Other distinctive features of the quartet are the first movement's persistent elaboration of its opening motif, the use of fugato in first movement and finale (which he avoids in his early piano sonatas and keyboard chamber music), the expressive use of dynamics, including crescendi and decrescendi, often leading to a sudden piano dynamic, and the prevalence of dramatic gestures at crucial structural points in all four movements.[3]

The Adagio is one of Beethoven's most eloquent D minor statements, along with its fraternal twin, the 6/8 Largo e mesto of the piano sonata op. 10 no. 3. While sketching some striking passages near the end of the movement Beethoven jotted down references to *Romeo and Juliet,* curiously in French. He writes these words for successive musical phrases: "il prend le tombeau," "dese[s]poir," "il se tue," and "les dernier soupirs," thus depicting Romeo at Juliet's tomb: his arrival, his despair, his suicide, and "the last sighs."[4] Reflecting Beethoven's love of Shakespeare, these allusions are confirmed by a remark attributed to Karl Amenda, Beethoven's close friend and the recipient of the first version of this quartet. Amenda reported that when he heard Beethoven play this slow movement (presumably at the piano), Amenda said, "It pictured for me two lovers parting," whereupon Beethoven said, "Good! I was thinking of the burial vault scene in *Romeo and Juliet.*"[5]

These notations may well link to Beethoven's lifelong dream of opera, only once realized in *Leonore/Fidelio,* a link that became explicit in his late quartets when in op. 130 he included an instrumental Cavatina, a type of opera aria.[6] But in the op. 18 Adagio his confinement of the Shakespearean references to his sketches and omission of them in the published version show his reluctance to provide explicit literary programs for his string quartets.

The Scherzo of op. 18 no. 1 resembles Haydn's most active and dynamic fast Menuetti, with alternating passages of clever quartet dialogue in extreme dynamics (including a *ppp* segment at mm. 45–63) and with masterly control of details, many of which were not present in the first version but emerged in Beethoven's revisions.[7] In the Trio two gestures stand in striking contrast: the first a hammering figure with octave leaps, the second a legato passage for the first violin against sustained chords in the lower voices.

The same dynamic energy pours over into the vigorous finale, a 2/4 Allegro (intensified from its original Allegretto) in sonata-rondo form that matches the first movement in length and complexity of figuration patterns and has its own contrapuntal episode in the middle section of the movement. The big coda, more than fifty measures in length, brilliantly grounds the whole quartet. The final measures, with their rousing two-note figures in the first violin (with the second shortened to a sixteenth plus rest instead of an eighth-note) and crescendo, could not have come from any Haydn or Mozart quartet.

MAIN MOTIF

The soft, furtive opening motif in the first two measures, familiar to every quartet player, was more original when new than most people realize. This highly profiled six-note turning motif in triple meter, which opens the quartet in "unison" (actually in a one-octave statement) and then runs through the whole movement, evokes other concise Beethovenian opening gestures whose contour and rhythmic shape remain etched in memory.[8] The four-note motto that opens the Fifth Symphony is the most famous example, but there are many others, whereas we can look long and hard through Haydn's and Mozart's quartets without finding an exact parallel. Especially rare is that this figure opens and closes on a downbeat in 3/4 meter. It sustains the tonic pitch F, adds the simple turning figure with adjacent notes, then arrives decisively on a downbeat quarter-note followed by two quarter-rests.[9] Because the initial melodic motion is minimal, the first clear harmonic implication for the work is its leap from F down to C, the dominant, at m. 2, then its repetition with change of arrival note to D at m. 4. The whole pattern of the movement emerges from this single figure. It permeates almost every large section, generates the first principal "theme" and first larger paragraph, and determines many subsidiary figures.

This F major first movement (313 mm.) is the longest in the op. 18 quartets and in its sectional proportions it could be a middle-period work. The exposition (114 mm.) is compressed and recomposed in the recapitulation (95 mm.); the development (64 mm.) is about half the length of the exposition; and the coda nearly matches the development.

Some features call for comment before we look at their origins in the sketches and early version. The most obvious is the saturation of the movement by the opening motif, but more important than its sheer recurrence is the variety of guises in which it appears. Thus, the motif (which I will call "M") appears in all but one segment of the exposition, each time in a different role:

Segment A, mm. 1–29
Basic exposition in the tonic; M is stated and elaborated so that its first five notes remain intact but appear on varied pitches, with many variants of the arrival.

Segment T1 (Transition 1), mm. 29–40
M is fixed as an ostinato in the bass, with new elaborative figures above.

Segment T2, mm. 41–56

The abrupt motion to A-flat major at m. 41 coincides with the shift of the ostinato pattern of M to the viola, along with new variants of M in violin 1. Especially telling are mm. 42 and 44–45 in the first violin part, where M appears first intact and then with only its last four notes. By this time the "turn figure" stands in for the whole motif.

Segment B, mm. 57–72

Here M is deliberately avoided to enhance the independence of the new theme in the dominant.

Segment C, mm. 72–83

The cello and violin 1 have a dialogue with two forms of M (the first is the ostinato form, the second is a new descending stepwise figure), then M yields to new figuration patterns.

Segment D, mm. 84–100

After a strongly articulated rising phrase and a sudden full-measure rest (m. 88), M returns to begin the answering cadence.

Segment E, mm. 101–114

Again the ostinato form of M dominates (cello, mm. 101–104), then is converted to sixteenth-note patterns that run to the end of the exposition.

The close parallel between Segment E of the exposition and T1 is a key to Beethoven's artful treatment of motivic and harmonic articulation, since the same pitches in the cello at mm. 31ff and 101ff have different harmonic roles, the first being in F major, the second in its dominant, C major. It is a telling example of the many ways in which motivic elaboration and the larger formal plan can interact. In Mozart and Haydn, as well as in some works by Beethoven, we find a fair number of expositions in which the closing theme is closely related to the opening theme (e.g., Mozart's A major quartet, K. 464), but this movement is unusual in that the closing segment of the exposition relates instead to an early transition segment which had established a special use of the main motif—namely, in ostinato.

From here on in the movement, M undergoes more transformations, but we will not trace them all. Important, however, is that the relation between segments T1 and E in the exposition disappears in the recapitulation, where T1 is suppressed in favor of a wholly rewritten opening at the big return to F major (mm. 179–198); T2 takes its place at 198. Also striking is the last-minute appearance of a new and lively form of M, with its turning figure on the downbeat, followed by eighth-note pairs, at the very end of the movement (mm. 310–312).

Variety and imagination enliven the many appearances of the motif throughout the movement; to say that the motif "saturates" the texture is too simple to suggest what is truly afoot. With this movement Beethoven's integration of motif and form, always apparent in the best of his earlier works, rises to a very high level.

REGISTER

One of Beethoven's familiar strategies is to begin a long Allegro first movement quietly with a clear-cut motivic idea and eventually come home to the tonic and the opening theme at the recapitulation with a forte or fortissimo version of the opening idea, often rescored to dramatize the difference.[10] The opening theme or motif will typically reappear with the voices spread among more octaves than at the beginning, so that the registral expansion dramatizes the formal moment. Here the opening statement is quietly announced in piano dynamic and in a middle-register one-octave span by all four instruments and restated at m. 9 in the same limited span, though now in forte. But when it eventually returns at the recapitulation (m. 179) it is not only in fortissimo but has expanded to three octaves, F to f^1, with the first violin up an octave and the cello down an octave from the original statement, capitalizing on the cello's resonant open C string for the arrival point at m. 180.

This climactic effect of the recapitulation is foreshadowed earlier in the movement, namely at the end of the first larger paragraph, at m. 29. The expository material from m. 1 to 29 shows a steady expansion of range, from the one-octave range of mm. 1–4 and 9–12, rising in the violin 1 gradually to reach the upper octave, above f^1, first in mm. 14–18 and then decisively in mm. 22–29, where it reaches the apex of the violin 1 part, f^2, and creates a full four octaves from top to bottom. This gradual expansion over 29 measures from one octave to four octaves is forward-looking for Beethoven in 1799–1801 and its dramatic potential will stay alive in his compositional thinking through the op. 59 quartets and down to his last works (op. 127 and beyond).

CONTRAST AND CONTINUITY

As we have seen, some of the primary contrasts in this movement emerge from the dramatization of register, but Beethoven creates variety in other ways while he pursues the larger continuity of the movement. One way is through shifting textures. From the "unison" of the opening to the end of the exposition, each thematic and harmonic segment has its own textural features. Thus, the transition at T1 (mm. 29–40) gives thematic functions to the outer voices, first violin and cello, while the two inner voices maintain the harmony through pulsating eighth-notes.

The similar pattern that begins Segment C (mm. 72–77) brings the cello into its intense high register (the only time the cello plays at this pitch in the movement) with the second violin and viola below it. Again, at Segment D (mm. 84–88), the reaffirmation of the dominant, C major, launches a rising pattern in eighth-note pairs, now omitting the cello—and the dramatic rest at 87–88, leaving the previous figure suspended, makes the resolution at 89 all the stronger. Then the whole pattern is repeated an octave higher, at 92–96, followed by another rest, but now instead of the expected C major, all four instruments shift abruptly to C minor in low register, dramatizing the cadence that will drive forward to a new goal at Segment E (mm. 101ff).

Much more extensive are the textural contrasts in the development and recapitulation. The development has four main segments:

Mm. 119–128, B-flat major—D minor. Here rapid one-measure contrasts use M and the two-note descending figure derived from m. 6, now at 124–125 and 127–128, in violin 1 and 2.

Mm. 129–150. A fugato, descending through minor keys on the circle of fifths (D–G–C–F).

Mm. 151–166. A steady "plateau" with pulsating middle voices and descending arpeggios using M in the first violin; B-flat minor—G-flat major—F minor—D-flat major, eventually resolving to the C major dominant that will prepare the recapitulation.

Mm. 167–178. The retransition strongly articulates the dominant harmony with rapid scales in both directions, syncopations, and offbeat accents. To cap the climactic effect, a crescendo at m. 178 prepares the fortissimo arrival at the recapitulation. The strongly accentuated character of this passage derives from earlier running sixteenth-note scalar passages (e.g., mm. 49–54, 78–81, and 109–112, which have locally climactic functions). But with its running scales in both directions, its strong rhythmic propulsion, syncopations, and offbeat accents, this passage just before the recapitulation stands out as the peak of highest tension in the movement.

THE SKETCHES

Beethoven had started work on the F major quartet at the end of Grasnick 1, as his first sketchbook came to be called, directly following extensive sketches for the D major quartet (op. 18 no. 3) and some other lesser pieces, but most of his work on the F major covers about thirty pages (16 folios) at the beginning of Grasnick 2, its continuation.[11] The outside dates for his work on both sketchbooks (which may have originally been one large volume, at some point divided in two) are mid-1798 to mid-1799.

Beethoven's decision to work in pre-assembled oblong sketchbooks rather than on loose leaves and bifolia coincided with his composing the op. 18 quartets.[12] As he embarked on string quartets for the first time, he clearly felt the need to proceed in a more orderly way than he could by using loose sheets and leaves.[13] Using a bound sketchbook enabled him to shift back and forth within a long and varied movement, and to keep track of his growing body of ideas in the course of his busy and sometimes chaotic daily life. Despite some excursions, he tended to work on one movement at a time, following the basic order of the movements within the finished work.

The first detailed study of the sketches for the first and last movements of op. 18 no. 1 and for the second movement of the G major quartet op. 18 no. 2 was made by Donald Greenfield in 1982.[14] Greenfield's work effectively superseded earlier transcriptions, corrected some inferences that had become established lore, and provided a much clearer idea of how Beethoven worked out all three movements. I follow Greenfield now in outlining what the sketches reveal about the genesis of the first movement.

In broad terms, Beethoven first discovered the opening idea, then put the exposition together in outline by writing partial continuity drafts, then proceeded to draft the exposition in full. As with some later works, including the *Eroica*'s first movement, he needed four drafts to reach the basic form and content for the exposition section. After that he worked up three drafts for the development, a set of sketches for the recapitulation, and last of all, the coda. By and large he moved through the segments of the work in their final order. This ordering allows us to trace his progress through the larger trajectory of the movement and follow its cumulative logic from beginning to end. We see him circling back at times to earlier sections, to fix details as new ideas poured forth. The concentration and intensity of the process is palpable from start to finish.

The first sketches form attempts to shape the opening motif that I am calling M. The earliest sketch for the opening idea is shown in

3tes in c mol[l]

Ex. 3. Early sketch for opening (Grasnick sketchbook 1, f. 37v, st. 1–2).

Example 3. Just before the entry appear the words "3tes in c mol[l]" ("the third in C minor"), which can't refer to this example since it is unambiguously in F major, but probably shows Beethoven thinking he might do something with a possible third quartet in C minor.

Example 3 raises questions we cannot answer but it is rich in implications. It seems unlikely that at this stage of his sketch work, just as he was finishing the planning for the D major quartet, Beethoven would have been thinking about a different quartet in F major—that is, really different from what became op. 18 no. 1. Written on two staves, lacking the turn figure and the direct arrival on C in m. 2, this entry might suggest a piano sonata opening, but it has enough in common with the final version of the motif M to persuade us that it really is a primordial version of that musical idea. It implies an F major opening in 3/4 that begins on pitch 1 and ends decisively on 5; moreover, it immediately repeats this figure up one step, on G now moving down to D. The basic idea in outline, and its ending points on C and D, remain in what became the motif M. So Beethoven's original idea for M included the basic pitch contour of the first subphrase, with its downward motion 1–5, its amplified repetition up one step, and its arrivals on 5 below and then on 6 below.

At the bottom of the same page is a sketch that represents an evolutionary step toward the final theme, but now Beethoven has altered the meter to 4/4, which remains the meter for as many as ten more short sketch entries.[15] We can take the first of these as a sample (ex. 4). This sketch has the initial F and E of M plus upper neighbor, though not yet the turn figure; but it does have the replication of the figure a step higher, and now shows for the first time the idea of a continuation at a higher register (m. 3). These elements will survive through all the experiments in 4/4 that follow, some of which were not intended to refashion the initial motif but seem to refer to other parts of the movement. A further sketch, still in 4/4, clearly foreshadows the ostinato use of the opening figure in the cello under further elaborations in the upper strings (which appears in the final version at mm. 29–36 and 101–104). This shows Beethoven, having fixed his initial motif, looking ahead to its use in one of the more dramatic situations in the movement (ex. 5).

A sketch on the next page, although still in 4/4, is the first attempt

Ex. 4. Early sketch for opening (Grasnick 1, f. 37r, st. 14).

Ex. 5. Early sketch in 4/4, showing initial motif in ostinato (Grasnick 1, f. 37v, st. 5–6).

Ex. 6. Early draft of exposition in 4/4 (Grasnick 1, f. 38r, st. 9–11).

Ex. 7. Early draft of exposition in 3/4 (Grasnick 1, f. 38v, st. 7–8).

at an exposition draft. The basic shape of the first phrase has now been fixed, extending out to eight measures, and, except for its phrase-closures at mm. 6-9 and 13-16, it is on the way to the final stage (ex. 6). Next is one of the earliest drafts in 3/4, which Beethoven definitively employed only after he had tried out a number of sketch passages in duple time (ex. 7).[16] The opening figure now fixes its grip on the phrase and on the movement as a whole. Still to come is the way of completing the first two phrases. The rapid descending arpeggio on the dominant seventh in m. 6 and its continuation are awkward by comparison with the smooth closing measures that Beethoven finally achieves, and so is its counterpart at mm. 14–15. As Greenfield points out, these ideas fail to resolve the motion from C to D in mm. 1–4.

Without pursuing the sketch process further (it awaits a fully detailed special study), we can summarize the main points.[17] Beethoven started out with uncertainty about meter but not about his initial motif, which he established early in the process. He looked forward to later phases of the exposition before he had made a final choice about the shape of the opening phrases. He needed four drafts in all to reach a satisfying version of the whole exposition, and by the fourth he was refining details laid down in the third. Some particulars draw notice: first, a minor-mode episode follows the structural arrival at the dominant, and the closing theme is more or less the same throughout the drafts. Second, as Greenfield notes, "Beethoven gave unrelenting attention to the main thematic unit (everything up to the big cadence preceding the modulating episode, corresponding to mm. 1–29 of the finished movement). Each rendition gained in complexity and interest, and a continuing effort was made to propel the music onward, beyond the point in the consequent phrase (around mm. 15–16 in the completed piece) where a cadence would occur if strict parallelism with the antecedent phrase were being maintained . . . the cadence, when it finally arrived, resolved quite an accumulation of tension."[18]

THE AMENDA VERSION AND THE FINAL VERSION

Among Beethoven's few close friends in these years—or any years—was the violinist and clergyman Karl Amenda (1771–1836). Originally from Courland (Latvia), he came to Vienna in the early months of 1798, first as tutor in the Lobkowitz household, then in that of Constanze Mozart.[19] In late June of 1799, when Amenda left Vienna to return to Courland, Beethoven gave him a manuscript copy of the F major quartet with a dedication signed "your true and warm friend" in which he declared that the parting gift was a "small testimonial of my friendship" and asked, "whenever you play it, think of the days we have lived together."[20]

Further correspondence between Beethoven and Amenda confirms their friendship. The most telling is Beethoven's letter of 1 July 1801, in which he nervously confessed his worries over his oncoming deafness, along with his distrust of his "Viennese friends" such as, perhaps, Schuppanzigh and Zmeskall. In need of support from a trusted confidant, he hoped, if his deafness were to worsen, that Amenda might be willing to "give up everything and come to me"—that is, return to Vienna and become his companion.[21] He ends the letter, "Be sure not to hand on your quartet to anybody, because I have revised it very thoroughly. For only now have I learned how to write quartets properly, as you will see when you receive them."[22]

This remark is confirmed by comparison of the two versions. For Amenda did not destroy the early version; it remained unknown until the late nineteenth century, when it was found among his posthumous papers. The first movement was published partially in 1904 and in full in 1922, and in the 1960s the score of the entire version was made available in reliable transcription.[23]

The survival of two complete versions of any Beethoven work is unusual. He made, or sanctioned, a number of arrangements of works for new combinations of instruments, including his revision of the wind octet (later op. 103) as his op. 4 string quintet, and his arrangement of the piano sonata op. 14 no. 1 as a string quartet in F major.

We also have a few works that he first finished and then extensively revised. The most substantial was the opera *Leonore* (1805), first revised in 1806, then again in 1814 as *Fidelio* (including its four overtures, among which *Leonore* Overture no. 2 was rewritten as no. 3). Other examples are the two parts of his op. 121, published separately in 1824 and 1825. One is the "Kakadu" variations for piano trio (op. 121a), undoubtedly an early work with a newly written introduction in Beethoven's late keyboard style. The other is the *Opferlied* (op. 121b), which he set as a solo song in 1794, published in 1808, and reset for soprano and choir with orchestra in 1824. Another modified arrangement was his own transcription of the Grosse Fuge for piano four-hands, made in 1826 to supersede an arrangement by a younger contemporary that Beethoven found wanting.[24]

Beethoven's alterations of the F major quartet are so numerous that to follow them in detail would require a book in itself—indeed, a book that Janet Levy has already provided for the first movement. Instead I will furnish an overview of some central issues.[25]

Alteration of lengths of sections and their harmonic content, with passages added or deleted

The Amenda version first movement is eight measures longer than the final version. This is because a C minor segment of this length originally appeared in the exposition after the principal second theme (B1) in the normal dominant key of C major. Noteworthy in B1 (in both versions) is its complete avoidance of the initial motif M in favor of new legato phrases that form two eight-measure periods, subdivided into two four-measure pairs. The new eighth-note figures introduced at m. 57 bring contrast to the movement and relax the urgent forward motion that has been built up so forcefully from the beginning.[26] Though Beethoven rescores B1 in the final version and improves its details, the two versions are not basically different in content.

The striking difference is that the Amenda version, after its clear C major passage, arrives decisively on C minor for a passage in piano dynamic that offers some of the same textural features as T1 (two accompanying parts pulsating, the upper strings with M in dialogue). This C minor passage rises through a crescendo to its final cadence (Amenda, mm. 79–80) and leads into passage C, a much more original segment in which the cello brings M in high register, answered in dialogue by violin 1. In the Amenda version the violin 1 answers are in legato sixteenth-notes (accompanied by sixteenths in the viola that are awkward to play), while in the final version (mm. 72–77) Beethoven sets M in both outer instruments, with eighth-note pulsations in the middle voices. What he accomplishes here is twofold: first, he eliminates the C minor segment, which had weakly continued the C major second subject (B1), and moves forward unambiguously in C major; and second, in the final version he uses the textural material of the deleted C minor passage in the C major passage (segment C), making the whole phrase more climactic and effective as a continuation of the second subject.

The other passages that are decisively recomposed are in the development and recapitulation. The development (Amenda mm. 123–184, final mm. 128–178) shows rewriting that improves the rhythmic flow, tightens the motivic and contrapuntal treatment, and intensifies the formal dynamics. An important change concerns the segment in contrapuntal imitation (Amenda mm. 137–157, final mm. 129–151). In the Amenda version the passage is set off by a measure rest (Amenda m. 136), a gap that is filled in the final version (m. 128), but the differences that follow are more significant.

Harmonically the Amenda version is laid out in this way: G minor (m. 129)–C minor (134)–F minor (149)–B-flat minor (155). Thus the earlier plan is to move down through the circle of fifths from G minor to B-flat minor, then continue with four-measure groups based successively on B-flat minor (m. 157), G-flat major (161), V7/F (165), and F minor (169), leading to the retransition on a firm dominant at 173. The final version instead begins the fugato in D minor (m. 129), then moves as follows: G minor (135)–C minor (141)–F minor (147)–B-flat minor (151)–G-flat major (155)–F minor (159)–D-flat major (163)–V/F (retransition, 167).

So the first part of this cycle moves from D minor through fifth intervals to the decisive change of texture in B-flat minor (151) that starts a new segment. By dividing it into two groups of eight measures rather than four groups of four, Beethoven lends it a longer breath. The two motions by thirds, from B-flat minor to G-flat major, and from F minor to D-flat major, grow logically from the downward-third motion that has been prominent in the movement from its very opening, when F moved down to D. In the final version the imitative writing is also more interesting. In the Amenda version the voices enter at one-measure intervals, rising in register from bottom to top (Amenda mm. 137–140), while in the final version the pattern is shifted by altering the order of the last two entries (mm. 129–131), compressing them into three measures and having the violin 2 enter on a syncopated second beat (m. 131), to break the symmetry.

In the recapitulation a significant revision follows the return of the opening thematic material in the tonic (Amenda mm. 185–202, final mm. 179–198). In the earlier version, a half-cadence on the tonic (Amenda m. 192) is followed by a motion to the supertonic G-flat major, which is then prolonged for nineteen measures (Amenda 202–220) before it resolves clearly back into F major. In the final version, a more complex elaboration appears. Now there is a series of half-cadences that successively tonicize scale degrees that have a role throughout the movement: I—flat VI—IV. The motion to G-flat major now seems more integrated because it is the logical result of a descending-third chain that begins from the tonic, and is an expansion of the implied descending-third pattern that started the movement. Moreover, the G-flat major segment is now reduced from nineteen to thirteen measures. The pattern is: F major (m. 179)—F: I–V (186)—D-flat: I–V (190)—B-flat minor (193)—G-flat major (198)—resolution to V/F (210). Thus in the final version the details and larger harmonic patterns connect more coherently than in the Amenda version, and they realize the potential of the material more convincingly.

Alteration of textural and idiomatic features

There are so many changes of texture that we could hardly list them all, let alone describe them in detail. One striking example will suffice: the retransition (Amenda mm. 173–184; final mm. 167–178). Here Beethoven is in process of whipping up excitement through intensified rhythmic action in fortissimo as he prepares the final muscular cadence that will bring the prolonged dominant to its tonic destination at the recapitulation.

In the earlier version the first simultaneous accent was at m. 177, and from here on the viola and cello continue in canonic imitation in descending scales, with effective use of the open C strings of both instruments. Above, the two violins hold measure-long notes of the dominant seventh, but with accents on each first beat (mm. 177–182). In the final version the basic idea is the same but all details are more sharply etched. Now the rapid sixteenth-note scales appear in three different instruments (mm. 167–175) and in both ascending and descending forms (at times simultaneously, a true Beethovenian fingerprint); the accents on the long held notes are not on downbeats but on offbeats (mm. 167–169, 171–174); and the first really simultaneous accent occurs at m. 175, coinciding precisely with the first violin's arrival at its highest pitch in the movement, a high B-flat, whereupon the contrapuntal texture dissolves over the next few measures to prepare for the long-awaited arrival on the tonic.

These examples help us understand why Beethoven told Amenda that "only now have I learned how to write quartets properly." How performers should approach the two versions (and there are, admittedly, some very beautiful details in the Amenda version that inevitably disappear in the final version) is taken up in the comments by the Juilliard Quartet.

CONVERSATION

JS: Joel Smirnoff (violin 1); **RC**: Ronald Copes (violin 2); **SR**: Samuel Rhodes (viola); **JK**: Joel Krosnick (cello); **LL**: Lewis Lockwood

SR The first thing, of course, is the principal motif of the movement, the motif on which the whole movement is built, in the first bar. How do you bow it? How do you get the expression of that particular enigmatic figure that will stand for the whole movement? We have tried many different bowings, starting both up-bow and down-bow in various combinations. It seemed to work best starting down-bow because that gives a natural inflection on the note that is like a diminuendo. The note breathes in a certain way. Then you have the two eighths on the third beat of the bar and the next downbeat up-bow, which gives them an upbeat feeling that helps to make the musical line carry over to the next motif. We continue that, especially in the soft places, all through the movement. Now, in the loud places, the forte in bar 9, for example, we play the last note of the motif, the first beat of bar 10, down-bow. We used to play that up-bow but we decided that maybe, because it's louder, there's a certain sense of resolution there, just a little bit more—and of course when it becomes fortissimo at the climax of the movement, at the recapitulation, we certainly do it down-bow to give the most emphasis possible and make it speak more vitally and evenly.

JK It winds up giving a very particular feel to that motif. And speaking as the cellist, all during it when the music goes on [*sings violin 1 mm. 30–31*] the cello has [*sings cello mm. 30–34*]. I know I'm very careful at all moments to give that kind of [*sings opening motif of Beethoven's Fifth Symphony*] feeling to this motif, and that's what's behind the bowing. It's just individual enough and peculiar enough to stand out in a crowd—and to stand for that motif which, as Sam says, has so much to do with the energy of this piece.

SR It keeps it lifted against other material that's a little more sustained, so it stands out in a particular way.

LL This is one of the earliest Beethoven works in which a single sharply defined motif followed by silence becomes the generating principle for the whole movement. It is a prime example of a progressive early Beethoven movement, in which the inner meaning of that idea has to be felt from the beginning as something crucial and then elaborated all through the piece.

JS You know, the first page of this work demonstrates already so much of what's going to happen with Beethoven's style. You've got the subito piano in bar 20, you've got sforzandi, you've got an ostinato in bar 28. Basically we're talking about one motif but the motif has various endings to it. It has one note [violin 1, mm. 1–2], it has a swell [mm. 13–14], and then it has sforzando [m. 22]. From my point of view, the difference in the ending of the figure each time dominates the way that you are going to play the first part of the figure. So in other words, we start with the very simple and then we go to an espressivo in bar 14, and then [*sings violin 1, m. 22*] and that to me dictates the character of how we play these things, and then we have the sforzandi. So he's taken something and examined it from many, many different angles already, very quickly, and that's the excitement of the piece for me.

RC In a way he's using different words: the swells, the sforzandi, and even the rests after the notes reflect those different words, those different syllables, so to speak.

LL There are two ways to look at a motif like this and its role through the movement. One is that it is a kind of anchor against which other things change, and the other is that it's like a character in a picaresque novel who gets into various situations but retains his identity throughout.

JK He retains his identity but it's not unchanging. On this very first page, there are four sforzandi in a row. Okay, so what's done about that? Does that imply crescendo? Does that imply—already, as Joel says, what's on the first page of this piece is sort of Beethoven's life—

RC   Beethoven's anguish. [*laughter*]

JS   There's a manifesto of a kind here.

JK   Because that moment of [*sings viola, mm. 21–24*], culminating in a forte. You did start it piano, so is there some possible implication?

JS   In all the coaching that we do and in all the playing that we do, it becomes so obvious that the sforzando has a different function in Haydn, Mozart, and Beethoven—totally different. The Haydn sforzando is there to draw one's attention to a note, but it does not specify necessarily even an accent. The Mozart sforzando is usually an espressivo of some kind. And here Beethoven has shown you very quickly the difference between a swell and a sforzando. And he is saying, "No, my sforzando is not the sforzando of Mozart, which would be a swell, my sforzando is a *sforzando* sforzando"—and this is a sforzando that we will then live with, more or less, for the rest of musical history.

SR   But it's something also that evolved in his mind, obviously, because in the first version the sforzandos are still swells—and so he was unsatisfied with the way that was played and he realized that something else needed to be done at that moment.

JK   And, of course, there is a problem even with those swells. Are those swells on the note? In the first version it doesn't look like that. So if in the later version he felt he could substitute the sforzando, then he is talking about the start of the note, but if you look at the first version it doesn't look like that.

LL There are many things in the early version that needed to be made idiomatic in the second version; he needed to achieve a higher degree of profile.

JK In the early version, it's quite clear that there are hairpins not on the downbeat. Now is that printer's business or what?

LL Well, the first version exists only in parts which he gave to a friend, who didn't destroy them as Beethoven requested, and that's why they came into the world. So it's the second version that represents the most careful, exact edition.

SR And yet we don't have the manuscript for that version.

LL No, that's right. We have no manuscripts for opus 18, but we have the early prints and we have some early copied parts. So the situation is still a little bit more ambiguous for some details than it is for later music, but it may not be crucially so.

Let me ask you to address yourselves to the C minor passage that gets taken out of the early version, because that's a drastic change. Measure 72 of the final version splices over where this passage was.

SR In general, the second version, the final version, is much more streamlined than the original. In just about every case, things are taken out rather than added—sections, particularly in the first movement; or figures are simplified, made a little bit more friendly to the string instrument as opposed to the keyboard; filler material is simplified and streamlined. This is one example of a section where once he took it out he didn't totally excise it: he actually uses the dialogue idea, which he didn't have in the first version, although he takes out the part in minor as I guess he thought that it was unnecessary. He had enough material for that section of the piece. And he combines the two, so the essence of what he wanted to say with that section is there.

I think anybody who is seriously interested in composition should study the two versions of opus 18 no. 1, from the standpoint of economy in writing. I'm sure writers do this all the time. They have ten pages and then when they really pare them down there are only two pages and you have a much more cogent and streamlined version.

Another factor that's involved with a lot of the omissions that he made in the final version was that he had in his mind, or at least he evolved in his mind, a much faster tempo. And if you have all this clever stuff in between, it only gets in the way and a performer will want to slow it down so he can play coherently.

JK Even at bar 80 of the early version, when he turns to C major and takes away the minor, there are things in there which are really far more complicated than the dialogue.

JS What he's done actually is to set the dialogue between the cello and the first fiddle that he had in the minor—in other words, he reorchestrated the minor to the major, basically, and got rid of the minor bars.

LL Well, the cello attack in a high register on the motif, in the final version at measure 72, did preexist in the early version, but it doesn't have the dramatic power because it arrives after a C minor passage instead of coming after a passage which has no basic motif in it.

JK And also in the final version it's got eighth-notes against it. In the earlier version Sam plays sixteenth-notes through the entire section.

SR And the answer is in sixteenth-notes in the first violin.

LL It's one example of drastic recomposition, no question. Beethoven says in his letter to his friend: Do not give out your quartet to anybody, because only now have I learned how to write a string quartet. So it's a moment in his life when a revelation has happened thanks to all this self-critical hard work.

JK And it's interesting that, as Sam says, basically it's streamlined and simplified. There is nothing in the final version that's more than what was in the earlier version. It's less, it's truncated, it's streamlined.

RC The interesting thing is how much really beautiful music there is.

JK Oh, yes.

SR In the early version, no question.

JK If I say it, everybody is going to say it's true, that we are a little more fond of the development section in the first version. [*laughter*] I mean, it's got really wonderful things in it.

LL It's a little more symmetrical too.

JK And if you listen, as we have, to the performance of it which will be in this volume, you would say, "Gee, it's a Beethoven quartet," and if it were what remained it would be 18 no. 1.

RC But I think it also speaks to what he was demanding of himself, and what he really felt he needed to do and was compelled to do was to take this work and give up some really wonderful, imaginative writing in order to gain something else.

LL Yes. It's a lesson about artistic choice and it's very powerful. You have to give a little to get the other thing.

RC In this case, I think he gave up a lot.

JK But even things like the dominant passage that leads to the second theme, eventually—in the original version in bar 86, as opposed to bar 78 in the final version, where you have this wonderful [*sings mm. 78–80*]—

LL Offbeat accents suddenly attacked with second beats sforzando.

JS Those are very likable.

There is something that occurred to me while I was preparing for this discussion: those composers who are scribblers and sketchers and emenders, like Beethoven, as opposed to some-one who throws it down on the page and doesn't want to see it ever again. I mean, in Dvorak's recapitulations he never looks backward. They're always so different from the original state-ments, and they're not emendations. He just didn't want to know. Because of all the various levels of sketching, eventually you come up with the possibility of abbreviation, aberrance, and distortion which you could never come up with if you just put down something which naturally occurred to you. So the end result with a sketching composer, or with an emending composer, is something which is kind of otherworldly—and I think this is a large part of Beethoven's game. The sketching process starts with something natural and simple and eventu-ally becomes something which, when you encounter it for the first time, seems very strange.

LL Even the basic motif undergoes a lot of change from its pri-mordial state, and it even passes through a period when he's thinking of putting the piece in 4/4—which would lose a lot of the rhythmic bite because of the prolongation of the first note of the measure. You have to wait for the action to start, for the turn.

RC Isn't the thought the other way around? He would gain that by going to 3/4.

LL But it wasn't originally in 4/4. It entered into a 4/4 phase and then went out again, almost as if the process itself had a kind of developmental shape.

JS Addressing the performance of any of the opus 18s, you're walking a tightrope, stylistically. In other words, you're coming from the world of Mozart and Haydn and you're entering a world, of course, politically which has changed so radically and so you're moving out of the royal court and into the street, to some extent. And there is a great awareness that when you play this music you've got to be able to move between two styles. One is your normal classical style, which will not go beyond a certain scope in terms of sound; and the other is that to Beethoven the quartet becomes a great receptacle for abstractionism, that is, what the players can or can't do no longer matters to him at all at a certain point. Of course, in opus 18 there is a lot of concertante style in the manner of the Prussian Quartets of Mozart. So the challenges are great: more than one style is demanded right away.

For example, in bar 22 there is a series of sforzandos culminating in a forte. You would not necessarily see that in Mozart.

Let's address one which we constantly are talking about. If you look at bar 97, you have again four sforzandos resulting in a fortissimo, which poses the question of how much crescendo are you going to make. But then you have the cadence in fortissimo [m. 100] and, of course, this is the cadence that leads into the tiny little codetta—the tag, basically, on the end of the exposition. So the question is, what is he looking for in this fortissimo? Specifically, in the context of the nineteenth century that you're entering, it seems he's looking for a sound which we haven't quite encountered before. And when we play that fortissimo cadence there is always someone in the group who says, "Oh, it should not be so rough," and then there's another person who says, "Yeah, but it's got to have . . ." This is the borderline right there. That cadence is the borderline of one style and another. You sit on the fence right there between the two styles.

JK And also approaching it with those sforzandi. You can see it's a crescendo, but what it is—in my score I wrote piano sforzando, mezzo-forte sforzando, forte sforzando, fortissimo sforzando. Now that doesn't exist anywhere to this point and he hasn't put it down exactly that way, but what other conclusion can you come to? We also say in that fortissimo, "Hey, we should take time"—"No, we shouldn't take time."

SR To carry this even a little farther, let's take the final version of the opening motif of the work, the most developed example of that. You have the very beginning in piano. It is enigmatic, a little fragment which you realize soon stands for the whole piece, in a way. Then you have a repetition in forte with the same registration. Then you have it at the recapitulation [m. 179], where the buildup has culminated into a fortissimo with the register of the quartet spread about as far as possible as it can go. Obviously it's reaching out to somewhere that people haven't tried to reach.

LL   And it's followed by a very elaborate modulation into remote keys that comes right away in both versions, but a little more coherent and well-patterned in the second.

SR   In the first version, the forte comes right away, in the ninth bar. He already has the cello down an octave in that version even though it's forte and not fortissimo. And then in the later version he realized that to make that fortissimo really stand out as *the* moment, he would keep the cello at the opening where it was, in the same register. It will be a little louder but not this kind of explosion that he wants later on.

RC   Very good. I think it's wonderful.

JK   And at bar 92 in the first version, he doesn't move the violin up an octave.

LL   This way of thinking survives into the middle period and even into the late period. In opus 130 it is of the essence—the dramatization of register affects the whole first movement.

SR   In 59/1 also. The very first phrase, the way that culminates, you have the full range of sound possible. It may be even more than is possible in a way—this striving for more than is possible.

JK   One other aspect of this movement: There are a few threats of crescendi to fortes before the second theme, and finally when there's a unison fortissimo as an enlarged orchestrational thing [m. 179], again it's something that Haydn and Mozart would not have done. I mean it's another world of dramatic intensity, as though it were an orchestra.

That's the place in the first version where it's rather difficult to play [mm. 117ff].

RC Awkward.

JS That would be fine on the piano, it's just not good on string instruments.

SR He probably heard people struggle with it and it slowed them down. He wanted more of a flow to the piece, a faster tempo, and he just altered it.

JS You know, this is an issue that every composer will have to deal with. The ability to write for quartet, or any other medium, has to do with finding music that can only be written for that medium and cannot be played by any other medium. And if you look as he goes along throughout his career, it becomes very obvious to him what he should do with the quartet because he could never do it anywhere else.

LL There is one and only one example of a piano sonata which he transcribed himself for quartet: opus 14 no. 1. He changes the key of E major to F major, so that the open strings of the viola and cello can do their job, transforms the material very subtly, and some of it is very interesting. It is more interesting, in fact, as a quartet for that reason: in the finale, motives suddenly jump out of the quartet which are only implied in the piano part.

But he also says in a letter to the publisher that only the composer can be the transcriber; Haydn and Mozart could do this, and he could do it. But no one knows of Haydn and Mozart transcribing piano sonatas for quartet. So I think he thought they could have. They would have been the right people to do it. But what he is saying is, "I am the one who has to do this." Beethoven goes to great pains to tell the publisher: "This is going to be done, I'll do it," and you can see from the result that it's very good.

Before we leave this piece, I would like to hear a little more about when you're coaching, say, a student quartet, and you're trying to get this point across about being on the border between the styles. How do you go about having them experience it?

JK Aside from anything else that Sam brought up earlier, really reading the music. If you really read the music you have to deal with four sforzandi that wind up at a fortissimo or a forte, you have to deal with the subito piano in bar 20.

RC At the same time, we've all run into students who will deal with that by playing [*sings m. 20 with abrupt drop in volume*], meaning not dealing with it in a way. And I think your point is to get people to enunciate this in such a way that we listeners hear it. Especially with Beethoven by this point, these are becoming signature aspects of his style and his personal voice.

JK This is certainly a place where I would have them take out the subito piano.

SR The tendency is to round off the corners and just play it smoothly. You do it like a hairpin. That's usually the first stage of it. The second stage is what you said: that you play it sort of grotesquely because you don't know technically how to handle that; you have to teach them or make them aware of how to handle it technically.

RC Is now a good time to talk about subito pianos, generally? This is something we want to make sure to get to.

JK In our versions of the scores, there is a consensus about what it is we do, but at any given moment dealing with the subito pianos depends upon the harmonic context, depends upon . . .

SR One of the biggest parts of any interpretive discussion of Beethoven would be the subito pianos. That's such an integral part of his style. And that's certainly one of the big issues when you teach these pieces to people who are not so familiar with reading music in that way, and with reading music in general—because Beethoven, especially in the middle and later works, is so specific about what he wants. He's the first composer like that. You have to read the music with its dynamics and expression marks to understand how those marks, if you follow them, will lead in a far-reaching way into the expression of the piece.

JK And yet those marks don't necessarily annihilate the meaning of a long phrase that would exist if those marks weren't there.

RC They can't.

JK One has a sort of counterpoint between the two. Very often one of the teaching devices is to take a long phrase like, for example, the opening of opus 130, and say, "Now, really sensitively and beautifully play this, and take out those dynamics." Okay, that's one truth. Then how do the subito pianos affect it?

LL Especially in that movement, crescendo to a piano, growth to a falling back, is of the essence, in all sorts of ways.

SR It's such an important hallmark of his style. Opus 130 is built on it.

JK If you read carefully in our editions, is it piano crescendo to piano or is it pianissimo crescendo to piano? There's a difference. There's one in particular at the end of the first movement of 130 where we choose to go to piano rather than above.

RC The subito piano is especially important because of the difficulties we had. We came to the decision when marking these scores that we would use a single marking—a comma with a slash through it—to reflect most subito pianos, and yet . . . [*laughter*] every subito piano in some respects is different and each time we come to it in different ways.

We wanted to make sure that this symbol didn't go into the book as something that would be obvious in and of itself, but rather as something that might point to an event to be enunciated. I think Beethoven often uses the subito piano partly to create a resistance to the easy flow of time. And so our task as performers is to realize that particular resistance—in that particular harmonic and dramatic context—and not simply to take time.

JK A typical example of what Ron is talking about is in the final version of 18/1 between measures 48 and 49. There's an event. One of the possibilities of trying to get students to understand it: you play that scherzando the way you would play it. And then back up for a moment and play [*sings phrase more emphatically*]. And then you get the hell out of the way and see what they do.

LL It reminds me a little of what you would expect a great actor to do with a Shakespearean speech, who sees ways of suddenly shifting the emphasis and the intensity unexpectedly, in a kind of counterpoint to the normal discourse.

JS Again I have to bring up the idea of the composer who goes back over and over and emends, because the big question becomes: Did Beethoven conceive of the phrase with the subito piano when he actually composed it, or did it come to him afterward?

LL Most of his manuscripts show a late pass through the content for the dynamics. But that's only when he wrote them down. So it's hard to say for sure, but at least we can be sure that he didn't set that up as an absolutely essential situation from the very beginning.

SR But for example, in the case of opus 130, the first movement, it seems to me the whole essence of movement is that. Right in the first two bars, so it must have been in his mind.

JK Even in that moment, what's interesting is that he slurs the cello through the subito piano, to sort of say: separate but not separate.

JS From my point of view, there are two issues that we actually haven't talked about relative to the subito piano which I think are relevant. One of them is that, as one goes through from the late eighteenth through the nineteenth century, composers are more and more specific about exactly what they want to hear from the players. You go to Haydn, there's nothing. You go to Mozart, there's more. You go to Beethoven, there is the beginning of this philosophy that we could describe any shape that we want to hear in sound, so that whenever this is performed it's going to have that shape. That's kind of a new idea and that also implies that maybe this piece will be played years from now rather than just today.

JK By somebody you would never have met.

JS That idea comes to the fore. The other is the possibility—and I throw this out just as a hypothesis that I don't even advocate, but just as a jumping-off point—that as capitalism develops, as individualism develops, society contains more and more tension. Just as we're inventing new means of production, we're also inventing newer and more fraught tension-raising mechanisms—until we finally get to the resolution. I don't know if this is true or not, but certainly in the case of Beethoven I don't think there's any question that the tension level is being raised from the classical period.

LL This is an immense subject, of course. There is a German historian named Reinhart Koselleck who's got the theory that, beginning with the start of the industrial revolution—as transport emerges, the steam engine emerges, people are going faster—issues of motion and time are much more intensified in general social experience than they had been earlier. There are people who have applied that idea throughout nineteenth-century art and music and culture.

JS So that the subito piano, in a way, becomes both a release and a relief from a tension—saying no, I don't want to be a part of that. There are many meanings we can attribute to the subito piano and, in my teaching, I'm always saying to my students: What do you think it means? What is it? What does it represent?

Psychologically, it has one very important meaning for me in terms of the development of the psyche, and that is as a reconsideration—the documentation of a stepping-back and saying: I'm of a different mind than I was one moment ago.

JK I often illustrate it with my students as a reaching out toward something and then pulling back.

JS But in terms of the development of the documentation of the human psyche which, of course, takes a big jump with Berlioz. [*laughs*] Huge! Things are happening really fast at this particular moment.

LL It takes a jump with this composer in ways most people don't know. In the sketches for the slow movement of this quartet are these unmistakable references to *Romeo and Juliet,* the tomb scene. *La Malinconia* [op. 18 no. 6, Finale] is the first classical quartet movement with a title that stipulates an emotional state; it remains a landmark in that way.

RC Apropos of subito piano and time, look at the sudden modulation to A-flat major in measure 41. The unexpectedness of that event creates the same kind of difficulty in time as the subito piano—not the same gesture, but the same kind of difficulty of an unexpected event and what it does to deflect a linear flow of time around it.

LL It is highly dramatic.

JK He didn't put anything there, but are you just going to run though the event as it occurs? It happens to have a side-slip that's really some deal.

SR That's why we marked it "melt into."

RC And added the wavy line. What I think is important is that in looking at the scores that are in this book and seeing something like this wavy line, it's not predominantly giving a sense of "take time." It's more of a sense of feeling some kind of resistance, or some kind of impending difficulty, which will *deflect* time. But if as performers we try to take time, it usually creates some kind of dissipation of tension. On the contrary this needs to be a building-up of tension.

JK Again, it's the sort of thing where you would have the student play that bar, in which the A-flat occurs, a couple of times and then have the student play bar 40 and stop; and then get out of the way and say okay, how do you get to the next bar? Because, as Ron says, the time you are going to take isn't for comfort.

JS I think that brings up a kind of rule which we have talked about in performance, which is one takes as little time as possible. In other words, the formula is: do it with the least possible that is still natural and that maintains the tension rather than lessens it.

JK With the specific point: is there an event to underline?

SR For example, the passage that Ron pointed out: if we look at the recapitulation [m. 198], it's even more extreme. We would definitely take more time at the crescendo and the subito piano. It leads you into a very remote key, the lowered second [G-flat major]. You find yourself almost in a world that's totally alien, looking around and not quite knowing where we are and how we got there. Just that emotion means that you have to take time to do that, you can't just go straight through it.

JS You know, vis-à-vis our marking of the scores in general, I think that something needs to be said. As quartet players of all this music from the mid-eighteenth century through today, we get very accustomed, because we play together all the time, to making certain kinds of shapes. In other words, when we look at a piece of music, we make very quick decisions and united decisions, or discussed decisions, about what shape every note should be. Basically you have two shapes in music: you have the crescendo and the decrescendo. You have the swell and the opposite, and you combine them to make other shapes. And a lot of the marking that you can see in our scores has to do with what shapes we decide to make, to make sense—to maintain the line, to make sure that a phrase illuminates the quality that Beethoven is looking for, and so on.

RC I would even go further and to say that very frequently what we tried to do, in sitting down to mark the scores, was to capture the most common experience that we have. But we realize that in doing this we seem to imply that there is only one way we play this. And I suspect that's not quite the truth. There are tendencies that we have in approaching these kinds of gestures; any one performance may have some of this or not. When composers have to, say, mark something rhythmically, they will come as close as they can to what they have in mind with the notation. We're doing the same thing.

JK For example, Sam is pointing out in the recapitulation at the same place [mm. 197–198]. Okay, we're going to outline this remote key area that's reached in bar 198. At the same time the cellist is allowed to say, "Hey, I have V–I to that." Depending upon, for example, where we are in performance, on how much sound there is on the stage and what you're hearing, you want to disconnect this in a way but you want to connect it in another way. The marking means we've had a discussion of this as an event: okay, but exactly what are we going to do about it?

RC In preparing these scores the intention was to give someone who is looking at interpreting these works, perhaps for the first time, an alert as to where we feel there are important events. The markings are an indication that you need to figure out what that event is about—not that you need to take time, or provide a breath, or . . .

JK Taking time done in a taking-time way has a way of sounding really not too interesting.

JS One more subject: I'm looking at the forte-piano in bar 239, another forte-piano in bar 245, and then I'm seeing the sforzandi in 258. For us there is a very clear difference between a forte-piano and a sforzando. The sforzando, of course, is a transparent marking—it could be in any dynamic—but the forte-piano specifically demands that there is a moment of forte. How long that is depends upon the gesture that one is playing, but there is a moment of forte. If you look at the sforzando in 258, the way that we play them, they start really in piano.

RC And in the first edition, those were sforzandos.

SR Well, it depends on the context always. The forte-piano in 245 is quite expressive, whereas the sforzandos in 258 are not really expressive. They're pinpoints.

JS Exactly.

SR Sometimes I think he's inconsistent in that, at least with fortes and sforzandos.

LL Working with a notation that is not as fine-tuned as he might want it to be?

JK Even the forte-pianos in 239 and 245 are very different kinds of forte-pianos.

JS But I just want to express it in general—if at first there is a very clear division between what is a forte-piano and a sforzando.

One more thing: there are a lot of pianissimi and piani in this movement. Here's a moment for you vis-à-vis our teaching: I had a guy who studied with Ron Copes, I believe [*general laughter*], who in the midst of a quartet coaching said, "Don't you agree, Mr. Smirnoff, that the distance between piano and pianissimo should be greater than the distance between any of the other dynamics?" And I thought about it and I said, "You're absolutely right!"—the reason being that it is very hard for the listener to distinguish between the two. One makes an extra effort to make a pianissimo something which has a very special whispered quality about it, and the idea of the pianissimo, as regularly as it appears in this piece, is a kind of new leaf in terms of quartet writing. I think one works harder to project a pianissimo in the hall than one works to project a fortissimo in the hall. The distance between piano and pianissimo, and between forte and fortissimo, is a very important aspect of successful performance of any of these pieces.

SR When we come to opus 59 no. 1, you can see a very clear realization of that, where he is consciously trying to expand the expressive possibilities of the quartet in both directions. And therefore those dynamics are important.

JK One more comment about making the difference between forte and fortissimo and piano and pianissimo in a piece like 18/1 that's this fast, this electric, this wild—it gives it that breathless quality. It could very easily flatten out and not have that.

SR Speaking of breathless quality, that brings us to something else that we have not discussed yet: the metronome markings.

JS And the resulting compression.

SR As I said before, part of the reason for streamlining the piece and making the events more playable is because he felt it in a faster tempo. When he came to metronomize this, much later on in his life after the metronome was invented and he realized its importance, of course by then he was deaf, pretty much. He didn't hear the actual sound, just what was in his head. He came to 54 to the bar for this movement. And that, as with many of his marks, is very fast.

LL The whole metronome marking story is a minefield of trouble, but it can be revealing.

JK You're certainly not going to ignore any information that comes from the creator that you can get. You know, students are always asking, "What about the metronome marks?" One session with Isaac Stern at his chamber music seminar in Jerusalem, we went through all kinds of metronome marks with groups that were studying the pieces, and as far as Mr. Stern was concerned: "Oh, come on, don't be ridiculous. You can't do these things that fast, you can't do it." The fact is literally you can't do them that fast, perhaps. What the markings indicate, as Sam is saying, is Beethoven's wanting a certain velocity, a certain sense of intensity.

You're not going to ignore something that may have an emotional implication from the guy who put it down. The difficulty is going back in his head, especially not hearing, at some distance. Clara Schumann did that, when after her husband died she was asked to make an edition. Some of the pieces she knew from firsthand and some not, but she of course had heard them all and she did it from memory, as it were. Some of them were a little strange. But it's a piece of the original information.

LL There is some interesting countervailing material from Beethoven also. There's a song in which he wrote a metronome marking and annotates it: "The following should be the metronome marking, but if the heart feels differently it's all right." [*laughter*]

JK And then one has period metronome marks. Czerny—

LL Czerny has lots of them. For the late quartets, we have them from Holz, who was the second violinist. It's a complicated matter.

JK Except, just don't dismiss it.

LL No, it gives you character and a mindset.

JK People say: Ah, you know, his metronome, it didn't work. He got confused, he wrote it twice too fast.

LL He published these metronome markings in 1817 for the symphonies up to that point, namely all but the Ninth, and the quartets up to that point, that is, through opus 95. And that's where we have them. So it's a hard thing to be sure about.

JK But the major thing all of us agree on is that one doesn't dismiss it—to say, ah, he was deaf.

LL Of course you are not going to dismiss such an important body of information.

JK One of the things I guess we bring to this is having worked with a lot of composers. Some very wonderful composers of today write a metronome marking and you can't do it; and then you come and you play it in a certain way, twenty points under the metronome marking, but with great intensity, and they say, "Oh, that's wonderful." I remember pointing this out to Dick Wernick once. "By the way," he said, "when you left, I changed the metronome marking."

SR But, as I was saying, about this metronome mark that Beethoven gave for this piece, it gives you an idea of the pulse—that it's one to the bar. That's very important. Even if you don't play 54, you play 52 or 50 and have that feel. It's obviously not in three, it's in one. There are other places where it's not so obvious.

LL You might consider analogous pieces where you have this tempo marking and this meter. There are not so many. If you look at Beethoven—I have gone through the whole body of the works from this point of view—the works that agree with this are the *Eroica,* and the opus 1 no. 3 piano trio. The piano trio also has an opening gesture with a silence following. So, it's what people are calling Beethoven's C minor mood, which isn't only in C minor. This piece has it too.

ANNOTATED SCORE

Opus 18 no. 1, first movement

From *Inside Beethoven's Quartets: History, Performance, Interpretation,* by Lewis Lockwood and the Juilliard String Quartet (Harvard University Press, 2008), copyright © 2008 by the President and Fellows of Harvard College.

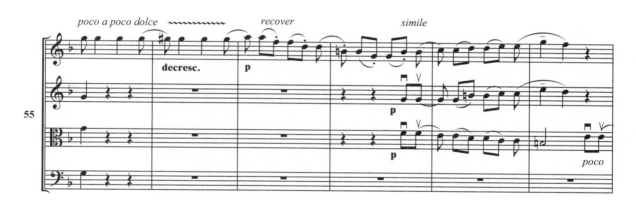

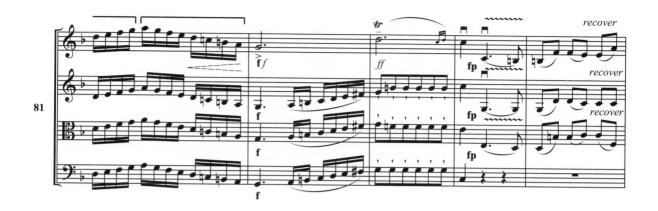

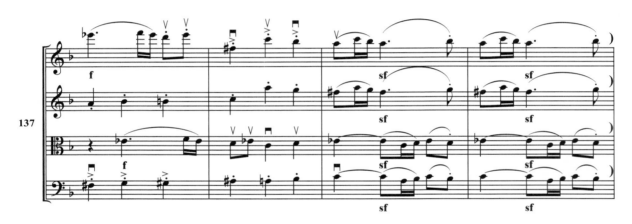

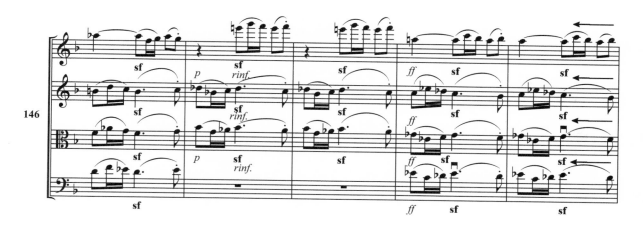

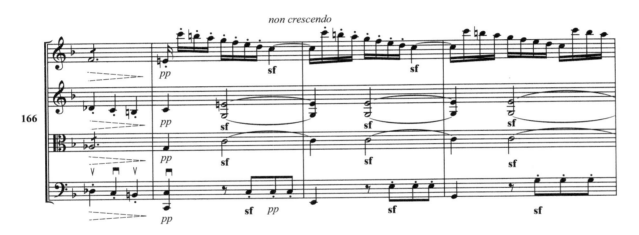

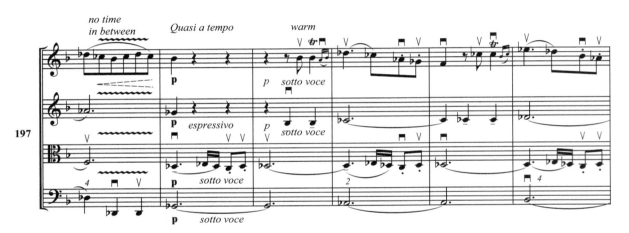

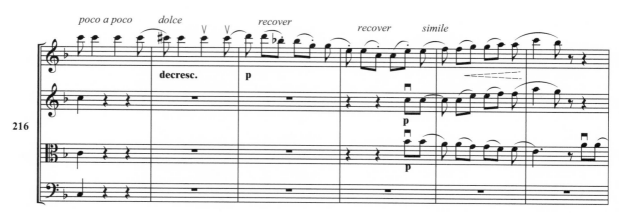

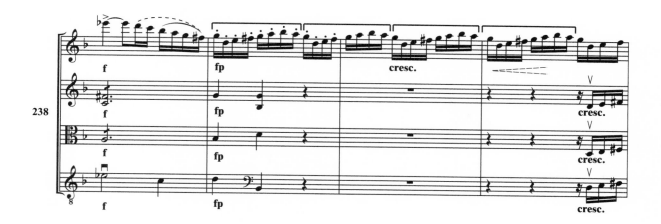

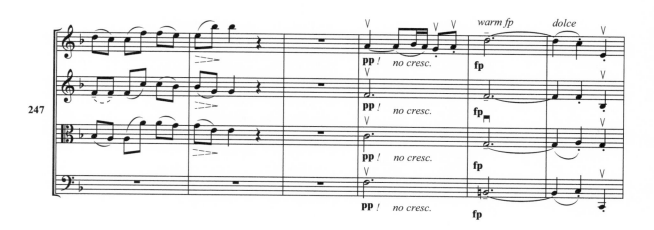

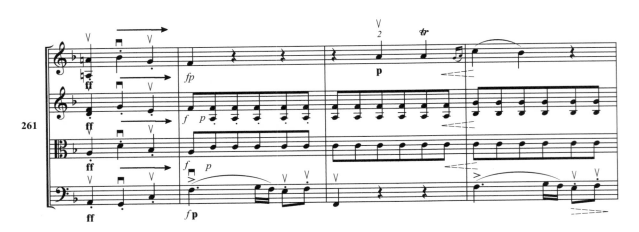

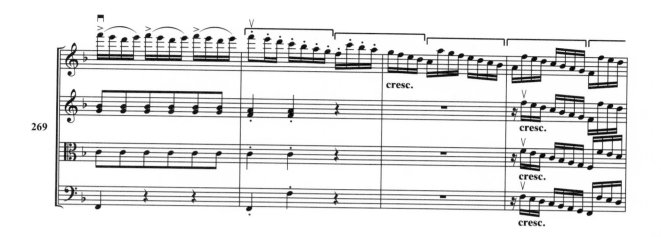

Opus 59 no. 1

THE "RAZUMOVSKY" QUARTETS

"They are not for you, they are for a later age," is Beethoven's alleged answer to the violinist Felix Radicati, who had complained that the three Razumovsky quartets of op. 59 were "not music."[1] Radicati was not alone. Adalbert Gyrowetz, then composer and conductor at the court theater, told a colleague who had bought a copy that he had "wasted his money."[2] And the famous cellist Bernhard Romberg, who had known Beethoven since their early days in Bonn, after playing the Scherzo of op. 59 no. 1, with its four-measure opening on the single note B-flat, trampled on the cello part.[3]

With these quartets of 1806, commissioned by Count Andrei Kirillovitch Razumovsky, the Russian ambassador to the Austrian court, Beethoven had entered another world. As original as his op. 18 quartets had been in 1801, they hovered between past and future, and in them astute listeners heard familiar echoes of late Haydn and Mozart along with much that was new, much that was charged with the restless energy that was the younger Beethoven's hallmark. But with op. 59 Beethoven catapulted the quartet genre into the new revolutionary domain he had created since 1803 with his Third Symphony, the "Waldstein" and "Appassionata" sonatas, and his opera *Leonore,* premiered in 1805. He had written the first two versions of *Leonore* in 1804–1806, just before his concentration on these quartets, and with these works and his new experience with operatic expression, he commanded a more powerful musical language. The op. 59 trilogy stood in relation to his op. 18 quartets somewhat as the "Waldstein" and "Appassionata" stood to his earlier piano sonatas. They opened up a new vision and established new paradigms that looked to the future, as his nineteenth-century successors understood. They embodied dynamic quartet writing that went far beyond the familiar and domestic sensibilities to which players and patrons had long been accustomed, and they moved the genre from the princely salon to the concert world.

As early as 1804, Beethoven's brother Carl wrote to the publishers Breitkopf und Härtel that if they placed an order for two or three quartets, Beethoven could supply them, though not right away.[4] But by July 1806 Beethoven could tell them that he had "already finished" one new quartet (op. 59 no. 1) and was planning more, adding, "I am thinking of devoting myself almost entirely to this type of composition." Two months later he was ready to offer them "three quartets."[5]

The autographs of all three quartets are preserved, but only a few sketches remain (the reverse of the situation with the sources for op. 18). The autograph of no. 1 bears the unusual inscription (in German) "Quartet begun on the 26th of May—1806."[6] All three manuscripts inform us about Beethoven's compositional process at a late stage of completion, though more remains to be gleaned from them than has been done so far.[7] The absence of sketches undoubtedly results from the loss of a major sketchbook for the year 1806. A few jottings for the last three movements of no. 1 appear on leaves now found in the so-called Mendelssohn sketchbook, which Beethoven used from mid-1804 to the fall of 1805, but these leaves are later than the bulk of the sketchbook and probably date from early 1806.[8]

Closely associated with op. 59 was the portly violinist Ignaz Schuppanzigh, who had known Beethoven for about ten years when the Razumovsky quartets were being composed. In 1804–1805 Schuppanzigh had re-established his quartet, with Joseph Mayseder as second violin, Anton Schreiber as violist, and the venerable Anton Kraft as cellist.[9] A few years later Count Razumovsky took over the patronage of the Schuppanzigh Quartet, and from about 1808 until 1814—when a fire destroyed his palace—Razumovsky's support of music and other cultural pursuits was the talk of Vienna, maintained despite war, French military occupations, and general economic troubles.[10] Prominent in diplomatic and social circles, Razumovsky liked to play second violin in chamber music. When he offered Beethoven the commission is uncertain, but it was probably sometime in 1805.[11]

The quartets are famous for their use of Russian melodies, overtly in nos. 1 and 2, in each of which the relevant theme is marked "Thème russe" in the score, and possibly in no. 3, though in that work we are not sure whether Beethoven actually used a Russian theme in the slow movement, or alluded to some melodic formulas familiar in Russian songs. Beethoven's use of these melodies was certainly a bow to his patron, but it was more than that. To find suitable themes of Russian origin Beethoven looked into a collection of Russian folk melodies edited by Ivan Prach and published in Saint Petersburg in 1790. He chose for his first quartet a G minor/B-flat major lament sung by a soldier on his return from the wars, marked Molto andante, in 2/4. Transformed in key, tempo, and character (he brought it into D minor/F major, Allegro), it became the main theme of the finale of op. 59 no. 1. His choice for the E minor quartet no. 2 was the celebrated melody in 3/4, "Glory Be to God in Heaven," the same tune Mussorgsky later used for the coronation scene in *Boris Godunov*. Beethoven used it in E major in the Trio of the Scherzo.

Beethoven's choice of the Russian theme for the finale of no. 1 could have been a springboard for the composition of the entire quartet. This would be analogous to his choice for the finale of the *Eroica* of his own theme in 2/4 that he had used earlier in the *Prometheus* ballet, in a contredanse, and for his large piano variations op. 35. In this symphony, created on a monumental scale, Beethoven showed that he could build a powerful finale on a disarmingly simple ballroom theme. In the op. 59 quartets that make use of Russian themes, Beethoven demonstrates that these works, which are comparably long and complex, could also connect with popular music.

Beethoven's many later settings of national songs, among the less well known of his works, indicate that his bid for artistic universality included an embrace of national folk traditions. This direction for music had been given authority by the eighteenth-century cultural historian and philosopher Johann Gottfried Herder, who thought the music of a nation and its "favorite tunes" displayed the "character of the people." Following Haydn, who had set dozens of Scottish songs, along with some from Wales and Ireland, Beethoven composed about 170 settings of folk melodies for solo voice or vocal ensemble with instrumental accompaniment. Besides Scottish and Irish songs he extended the geographic range to include tunes from Denmark, Germany, the Tyrol, Venice, Poland, Spain, Russia, the Ukraine, Sweden, Switzerland, and Hungary.[12]

Beethoven's age was one of incessant war and invasion, from the French Revolution and its aftermath to Napoleon's campaigns across Europe. As French armies marched through the continent, Napoleon's administrators brought political and social change to their newly conquered territories in the German states, the Austro-Hungarian empire, Poland, Italy, and elsewhere. Successive military coalitions were raised against France by the greater European powers—England, Austria, Prussia, and Russia—plunging Europe into more than twenty years of military struggle that ended with Napoleon's downfall at Waterloo in 1815.

Among the cultural responses to war and turmoil was the rise of patriotic music, including national anthems. "God Save the King," the British anthem, dated back to 1745. Haydn gave Austria its "Kaiserhymn" in 1797 (with the text "Gott erhalte Franz den Kaiser," later "Deutschland, Deutschland über Alles"), a response to the "Marseillaise" of 1792, the French military marching song that became the masterpiece of the genre. There is a parallel between the "Thème russe" in the finale of op. 59 no. 1 and Haydn's use of his own great national hymn for the slow movement of his quartet op. 76 no. 3, also from 1797. Beethoven, well aware of national currents, had already composed variations on both "God Save the King" and "Rule Britannia." In 1809 he sketched a new Austrian military marching song, significantly entitled "Oesterreich über Alles," with words by his friend Heinrich von Collin, author of the play *Coriolan;* and in 1813 he celebrated the Duke of Wellington's triumph over the French at Vittoria with his *Wellington's Victory.*[13]

Although op. 59 forms a traditional grouping of three quartets, the trilogy differs profoundly from earlier quartet *opera* and has more in common with Beethoven's groupings of other works. Somewhere behind op. 59 lurk Mozart's famous last three symphonies (nos. 39, 40, and 41), composed in 1788, of which the last, the so-called Jupiter, is a glowing C major work with a contrapuntal finale, as is op. 59 no. 3.[14] But Beethoven's own stepping-stones include earlier sets of three: his piano sonatas (opp. 2, 10, and 31), violin sonatas (op. 30), piano trios (op. 1), and string trios (op. 9). That he followed this pattern even in his later career is shown by the late piano sonatas opp. 109, 110, and 111. His works also yield some "hidden" trilogies, among them the two piano trios op. 70 plus the cello sonata op. 69. In addition, paired compositions—"doubles" in the Romantic sense, which juxtapose two very different works—appear throughout his career.

No members of any Beethoven trilogy are more sharply contrasted than these quartets. The first is conceived on an expanded scale in each of its four movements, while no. 2, in E minor, is a work of visionary originality and in Beethoven's last period was still difficult for listeners to comprehend. Number 3, in C major, contrasts most strongly with its companions and seems to return to the classical scale of late Haydn and Mozart, with some Mozartian reminiscences.[15]

The E minor quartet no. 2 is pervaded by a sense of existential struggle, beginning with its abrupt opening gesture of two chords, forte, first tonic then dominant, followed by a full measure of silence. The continuation in pianissimo brings the first melodic material of the movement, then another silence and a sudden move to F major (the Neapolitan harmony, or flat II) for a full repetition of the opening melodic gesture—and then another silence! The discontinuous succession of new ideas creates a sense of tightly organized concentration, compactness, and contrast. And after the beautiful slow movement and jagged Scherzo have run their course, the finale begins with a strong harmonic displacement, opening not in E minor but in C major, denying the expected tonic for many measures until the shifts between C major and elements of E minor finally bring an arrival on the tonic E minor, the primary key of the movement, at m. 52 (well into the 409 total measures of the movement). The struggle between E minor and C major then resumes for much of the remainder, resolving only in the Più presto coda, where E minor eventually triumphs. This sense of hard-won necessity distantly anticipates, not thematically but aesthetically, the enigmatic question that Beethoven raises in the finale of op. 135, his last quartet—"Muss es sein?" ("Must it be?")—to which he gives the equally enigmatic answer "Es muss sein!" ("It must be!").

After the great breadth of no. 1 and the intensity of no. 2, the third quartet, in C major, has always seemed like a relief, and indeed contemporaries welcomed it as such. Thus an oft-quoted review in the *Allgemeine Musikalische Zeitung* for 1807: "three new, very long, and difficult Beethoven quartets [have appeared] . . . and are attracting the attention of all connoisseurs. They are deeply thought through and well worked out, but not comprehensible to everyone, with the exception of the last, in C major, which in its idiosyncrasies, melody, and harmonic strength must win the approval of every seasoned friend of music."[16]

That a primary model for no. 3 was Mozart's "Dissonant" Quartet, K. 465, in the same key (and which also ends a cycle) has been apparent for a long time. The relationship is visible from the outset, when Beethoven opens his quartet with a mysterious and harmonically ambiguous slow introduction, which wanders through uncertain harmonic regions before it finally arrives, after 29 measures in Andante, at a clear dominant of the tonic C major, to which it firmly resolves as the Allegro begins. Some of the figuration patterns Beethoven used for the first movement resemble some of those in K. 465.[17] The presence of a graceful Menuetto instead of a dynamic Scherzo also looks back to Mozart and Haydn, and the contrapuntal "fugal finale" (though it also has clear sonata-form features) inevitably evokes memories of Haydn's op. 20 quartets as well as Mozart's quasi-fugal finale to his G major quartet K. 387, the first of the six dedicated to Haydn. Beethoven had copied out the finale of K. 387, no doubt to study it, in earlier years.

But in other ways no. 3 is just as forward-looking as its companions, despite its classicizing features. The slow movement is a dark, expressive A minor 6/8 Andante that uses pizzicato to introduce a highly charged melodic bass line (a prominent feature of op. 59 and of Beethoven's middle period as a whole). Here the pizzicato at the opening tolls like a bell in the deep bass register, then gradually becomes melodic (mm. 5–11) before changing to *arco* and joining the higher voices. The slow introduction, for all its resemblance to that of Mozart's "Dissonant" Quartet, has a close kinship to the slow introduction to Beethoven's *Leonore* Overtures nos. 2 and 3, and even more to the strange slow introduction to the opera's "dungeon scene," in which the harmonic framework depends on the placement of three successive diminished-seventh chords.[18] Beethoven's way of composing out the implications of this slow introduction later in the Allegro, just before the recapitulation, looks forward to his later works. And so do the unrelenting passion and energy of the finale, a virtual *perpetuum mobile,* for which he later imagined a metronome marking (whole note = 84) that few quartets have ever been able to play with clarity and full command.[19]

THE FIRST MOVEMENT

At the opening of op. 59 no. 1 the cello in baritone register sings a pair of balanced melodic phrases below pulsating middle parts, opening up a musical space of seemingly unbounded lyricism and breadth. Then the first violin enters to take over the melodic lead, with the steady pulsation in the trio below, eventually arriving at a firm cadence in F major after nineteen measures. The whole passage conveys a feeling of growth and expansion unparalleled in the quartet literature up to this time, and indeed largeness of gesture is to be the hallmark of the entire work. Keeping the whole in view, as Beethoven himself once said it was his custom to do, we are struck by the outsized dimensions of its four long sonata-form movements. In this work Beethoven takes giant steps to create a new artistic image of the genre.

A common observation is that the op. 59 trilogy shows the quartet becoming "orchestral," closer to the symphony, which Beethoven had recently transformed in the *Eroica*. But op. 59, for all its size and weight, still retains the personal expressive qualities of chamber music—even though these works were no longer easily playable by amateurs. Despite their length, complexity, technical challenges, and strongly contrasted styles, the three Razumovsky quartets still belong to Beethoven's most intimate and heartfelt sphere of expression.

Here is the movement plan of the first quartet:

1. Allegro, 4/4, F major, 400 mm.

This vast sonata-form movement's shape marks a turning point in the history of classical quartet first-movement form because it has no repeat sign for the exposition but passes directly into the development section. Questions of formal proportion and length lay behind Beethoven's decisions about repeats. In his autograph manuscript he makes clear that the exposition is to have no repeat: he writes "la prima parte solamente una volta" ("the first part only once").[1] At this stage of composition he also planned to repeat the entire development and recapitulation—"la seconda parte due volte" ("the second part twice") was his marking in the autograph—but he later canceled the second repeat, no doubt because it would have made the "seconda parte" enormous in relation to both the exposition and the coda. Had he kept the plan to repeat it, the coda would have shrunk to less than one-tenth the length of the whole movement, which would be very far from the normal proportions of Beethoven's works.[2]

2. Allegretto vivace e sempre scherzando, 3/8, B-flat major, 476 mm.

Beethoven's largest quartet Scherzo to date, it is the only one that lacks a completely separate Trio. Like the first movement it was subjected to large-scale changes before reaching its final form, as we see from Beethoven's autograph manuscript, in which he first inserted an enormous repeat of almost half the length of the movement, then removed the repeat when he saw how gigantic it would become.[3]

3. Adagio molto e mesto, F minor, 2/4, 132 mm.
"Mesto" ("mournful") in the tragic key of F minor signifies an intense sadness bordering on grief, relieved only briefly in the middle section (at the D-flat major passage, mm. 72–79).

4. Allegro, F major, 2/4, 328 mm.
The opening *Thème russe* launches a powerful and energetic finale that grounds the whole work. Like the first movement and the Scherzo, the finale was altered at a late stage in the autograph, when Beethoven excised a long repeat near the end (mm. 287–325). In contrast to the gradual development of ideas in the first movement, this movement rapidly and dynamically elaborates its opening material through a sonata-form plan, with brilliant interplay in all registers. The Adagio ma non troppo interruption near the end suggests the original lamenting character of the original *Thème russe* in Ivan Prach's song collection, though it also serves as a moment of contemplation just before the presto conclusion whips the movement to its end.

FIRST MOVEMENT: FORM AND FEELING

Opening

Beginning an Allegro first movement with pulsating eighth-notes in inner voices in 4/4 meter had been the primary feature of well-known masterpieces including Haydn's C major Quartet op. 33 no. 3 and Mozart's "Dissonant" Quartet K. 465 and C major String Quintet

K. 515. Beethoven had recently used it in his "Waldstein" sonata, but had rarely employed it elsewhere.[4] In Beethoven's opening, though, listeners who might have expected such an accompaniment to support an opening melody in the first violin, or perhaps, an arpeggiated opening theme (as in K. 515), instead encountered an intricate eight-measure theme that is a milestone in Beethoven's use of a sustained melodic line in bass register.[5]

Moreover, the opening theme is one of those apparently seamless Beethoven first themes which contain motives that he can detach for development later in the movement (ex. 1). The theme begins on the tonic harmony in its least stable form, that is, in second inversion, with C in the bass; and there will not be a decisive arrival on the tonic pitch F until m. 19. The answering phrase (mm. 5–8) is an elaboration, not a simple repetition. Traditional means of launching an exposition seem far from Beethoven's mind as he brings developmental procedures into play as early as possible and keeps them going to the end. The second phrase emphasizes its initial pitch, D, as parallel to the opening pitch, C, setting up a step relationship, C-D, that will have long-range structural consequences for the movement and that relates to the *Thème russe,* from which it probably derives.

In several ways the opening is emblematic of all that follows. The

Ex. 1. Opening theme with motives marked.

first is its dramatization of register. The opening presents the main theme with a vertical span of only one octave. From m. 1, in piano dynamic with pulsating eighth-notes, to the first great climax at m. 19, there is gradual growth in several dimensions: expansion of the total pitch space, from one octave to four octaves; motion from the contextually unstable tonic triad to the firm arrival at a root-position tonic chord; and a shift from the *mezzoforte e dolce* dynamic of the first measure to a crescendo at mm. 6–7, which draws back momentarily at the sudden piano at m. 8, then resumes the crescendo at m. 13 (now in all four instruments, for the first time) and intensifies through forte to fortissimo.[6]

The feeling of dynamic growth emerges from the thematic material itself, first in the sinuous winding of the first phrase around the pitch C, then in the organically related reappearance of its first four notes, C–D–E–F, rising in whole notes in mm. 16–19 in violin 1, an augmentation that reinforces the cadence. The expansion of range in the opening measures can be instructively compared with the opening of op. 18 no. 1, first movement.

Exposition

Once the opening has reached the first tonic arrival at m. 19, the exposition continues through m. 102 with thematic ideas that belong to a world apart from Beethoven's early works. Progress is now by means of gradual transformation rather than abrupt contrasts. To fill out the detail of this development would require a close study of thematic sequencing in earlier Beethoven, which cannot be done here, but the basic differences between this exposition and that of op. 18 no. 1 are clear.

To see the overall form of the movement, I have divided it into eight segments, using letter symbols for musical material (T = transition; MT = main theme).[7] This approach focuses on the movement's segments in their actual succession, thus highlighting aspects of each segment that performers need to be aware of and whose features they can try to project in performance.

A1 (mm. 1–19). Each motif embedded in the main theme is distinguished by intervallic and rhythmic properties, spatial and temporal, and both kinds of properties will play a vital role throughout the movement (see ex. 1).

A2 (19–29). Derived from motif *o* of MT in new rhythmic form; the movement's first chromatic progressions are at 24–27.

T1 (30–47). New legato figures in the violins emerge over sustained tonic harmony in the lower parts; derived from motive *n* of MT, and with a new motive, *p,* at 33, important later. The autograph slurs mm. 31-33/1 in violin 1 and 2, and does the same in the lower strings in 34-37/1. Triplet eighth-notes emerge for the first time at 43, and the whole segment closes with significant downward scalar motion in violin 1, 42–44, then returns upward with the expansion of the original motif *m.* The harmony is moving toward the dominant; another long slur in violin 1 spans mm. 44-48/1.

T2 (48–59). Poised on V of V, the cello brings a new theme derived by diminution from MT, then descends chromatically from C to G at

53–58 while another new figure (four clipped eighth-notes) emerges in violins 1 and 2.

B1 (60–70). This new theme is as close as the movement comes to a principal second subject, now firmly in the dominant, C major. It presents a new legato lyrical theme in low register plus an elaborated repeat (60–62 and 64–66) in higher register. A new closing figure for this segment emerges at mm. 67–70.

B2 (71–84). Poised in high register for all instruments, triplets reappear at 73ff with new figures, resuming the sustained-note texture in the cello at 77ff; triplets then dominate the close of the segment.

B3 (85–90). We now come to the strangest moment in the exposition, with half-note chords at 85–88 echoing in high and low registers, alternating unresolved dominant-seventh harmonies of D minor and C major (hinting at the C-D contrast of the opening theme), then in forte at mm. 89–90, forming a blocklike summation, again in D minor, that leads to the dominant of C. This passage will appear twice more in the movement, always approached from fortissimo arpeggios in all parts and always beginning in sudden piano dynamic. (It thus can be seen as a long range echo of the sudden piano at m. 8 that follows the first crescendo in the movement.) These episodes sharply interrupt the smoothly flowing motion of the work with condensed, powerful, enigmatic chords in immediate registral opposition.[8]

C (91–102). The end of the exposition resumes the smooth stepwise motion of MT and of B1, combining intervallic features of both, and brings still another new figure, introduced by the violin 1 at m. 94 and taken up by violin 2 and viola in 95, cello in 97, and so on. This figure, which I call *m³,* is a diminution of m. 1 of the work and has affinities to earlier eighth-note figures (e.g., 33); it will serve for elaboration in the oncoming development.

Development

D (103–111). By returning to the first four measures of the main theme, Beethoven deceptively implies that he is repeating the exposition, then shifts course. With the arrival at the unexpected G-flat at m. 108 it begins to be clear that he is on a path to unknown destinations. The figure *m³* at m. 107 that leads to the G-flat, with its paired eighth-notes (two slurred, two dotted) is now deployed as a motif in the early part of the development section.

E (112–125). With a decisive move to B-flat major at 112, the development takes off. Combining familiar features (the pulsating eighths, the triplet arpeggios, and the main theme in full with altered intervals), the basic motion is from B-flat major to G minor.

F (126–143). Further motion through the circle of fifths brings articulations of D minor (130ff), diminished-seventh harmonies, and again G minor, leading to a less than stable arrival on E-flat as flat VI of G minor (139ff), all using the *n* figure of the main theme.

G (144–151). Return of the enigmatic half-notes in high and low registers, now for eight measures instead of six as before, moving through unstable diminished-seventh harmonies to imply B-flat minor (flat IV of F) moving to V/6 of F, thus hinting at a possible return of the tonic F major.

H (152–184). Instead of a return to F major, sustained harmonies in the three lower parts underpin discursive expansions in violin

1, using a variant of the *n* motif from the main theme, and eventually arriving at a well-articulated D-flat major (mm. 175–180), then abruptly shifting to E-flat minor (m. 184).

I (185–221). A long fugato in E-flat minor with further extensions to other points of harmonic arrival, finally arriving at F minor (mm. 203ff). The fugato is based on a new subject (violin 2, 185–189) with the now-familiar *m³* figure as its countersubject. By far the most evocative portion of the development, marked *sempre pp*, the fugato gives further depth to a movement that has made the exploration of tonal space a basic formal priority.[9] After the fugato, a phase of relaxation sets in (mm. 210–222), in which syncopated half-notes descend through a linearized diminished seventh to reach the dominant of C, resolving to C (the real dominant) to finally end the very long development.

J (222–242). The retransition, essentially based in the dominant, C major, again employs the legato triplet figures from B2 in the exposition. The action gathers momentum to ascend through scalar triplets to reach the high C at m 242, signaling the start of the recapitulation.

Recapitulation

K [= A2] (242–279). The recapitulation begins not with the main theme, A1, but, in a surprising reversal, with its original continuation, A2. Registral considerations are primary: the high C at m. 242, the apex of the movement's upper line, is left hanging at this great height as the violin 1 leaps down two and a half octaves (m. 242, last beat) and then prepares for another rise that will make possible the return of the main theme. That return is approached by another abrupt shift of register, now in the cello (252–253), with a sudden attack on the instrument's open C string, the lowest possible note in any string quartet. Then the cello makes its own scalar rise to reach the right tessitura for the opening theme at 254, while the violin 1 is still descending. The ensemble returns to the one-octave span that has not been heard since the beginning of the movement and the opening of the development section. Yet soon the harmony veers off in still another direction as it turns toward G-flat in m. 269, moving decisively toward D-flat major, with new extensions at 266ff.

T1 (279–294). The original material but now in D-flat major, and with another long extension at 287ff.

T2 (295–306). The reinforcement of mm. 295–299 by both viola and cello is the main difference from the exposition.

B1 (307–331). Rescored, the viola is now the leading voice. New triplets enrich the texture as the violin 1 soars once more into its highest register, briefly recapturing (at m. 318) the high C that was left hanging at m. 242. The fate of this note is one of the primary dramas in the movement, and as the section continues to recapitulate earlier material, now in the tonic, the same apex is reached again at 331.

B3 (332–337). The last appearance of the mysterious half-note passage, now beginning on the same high C and brought back to its six-measure length as in the exposition.

C (338–367). Now comes the climax of the recapitulation and the dynamic high point of the movement. Powerful bass support (with double-stops in the cello) on the dominant and then the tonic at mm. 338ff underpins the closing theme in violin 1, and builds through sequential repetitions of m^3 to the movement's strongest point of arrival: the main theme finally stated in high register, with full bass support on the tonic in root position for the first time in the entire movement (mm. 348ff). Yet this too is quickly undercut by the B-natural in the cello at 351, preparing the last phases of the movement. This part of the recapitulation is one of the most powerful altered restatements in Beethoven's works.[10]

Coda (368–400). The coda, like the development and even the recapitulation, begins on a contextually unstable harmony rather than in root position, thus preparing the further extensions that will lead to the final cadence. Once more, triplet figures prepare the main theme and then surround it as it re-emerges quietly in the viola and cello at m. 373, setting up another rising surge through middle and upper registers that leads to the last and most important return of the highest pitch in the movement. Once achieved, this pitch is sustained for five and a quarter measures, serenely presiding over main theme and legato triplet figures below. The sustaining of the high C coincides with the cello's once more reaching down to its open C string (in mm. 388 and 390), so that this quiet final climax brings the quartet to five full octaves from top to bottom—just about the maximum registral span available to the string quartet.

There will be more to say about this great passage, but for now we see Beethoven gently and clearly closing the movement at 391–393 by resuming the descending scales in the violin 1 with which he had started the recapitulation, all now recollected in tranquility. A last expansion through the registral space brings the final crescendo and the last cadence, a decisive V-I, delivering the closure for which the listener has long been waiting.

REGISTER

The essential role of register in the first movement has been the subject of much analytic discussion.[11] We can now go a step further by focusing on the movement's use of not only high-register peaks but also both high- and low-register extremes, and on Beethoven's ways of dramatizing those extremes.

The first way is by gradual incremental exploration of registral spaces, especially by moving step-by-step from middle to very high registers. This is a primary feature of the opening section of the movement, where the range expands from one to four octaves. Structural parallels to this opening segment reappear at well-defined later moments in the movement, as the upper line rises in mm. 44–48, 167–174, 234–242, 343–348, and 378–386.

Beethoven's second way of dramatizing extremes is by sudden, immediate juxtapositions of very high and low (or middle-register) notes, especially in a single instrument but also across the ensemble. Significant occurrences are at m. 19, violin 1; and mm. 85-90 (= section B3) and its two parallel passages (144–151 and 332–367), with their drastic registral attacks. At m. 242 (the arrival at the recapitulation), the reversal of the opening segments to start the recapitulation enables Beethoven to recall the dramatic effect of m. 19 and thus to give maximum stress to this drop of almost three octaves in violin 1. In mm. 252–253, the cello suddenly drops almost three octaves; and in mm. 362–363, the sudden fall in violin 1 reduces the tension as the recapitulation ends and the coda begins.

Important too is Beethoven's way of combining scalar descent and ascent in the same passage. This occurs at mm. 253–254, at the return of the main theme in the recapitulation, with scales descending in violin 1 and rising in the cello, to arrive at the single-octave span for the main theme. To clinch the importance of this last passage for the movement as a whole, we can look once more at the ending of the movement, where a sense of tranquil expansion prepares the way for the final cadence. The apex, as we have seen, is at mm. 386–391, where the high C, reached for the last time, is sustained by violin 1 for five measures and a beat before beginning its stepwise descent (parallel to the one at 252–254). But in the autograph manuscript of the movement we find that Beethoven originally had a different idea about this passage, in fact three different ideas.

At a very late stage of work on the movement, Beethoven first has the violin 1 reach C at m. 386 and hold it for one and a quarter measures, then begin the descent in m. 387 (ex. 2a). Apparently dissatisfied with the short extension of the high note, he rewrote the passage in the autograph (in the same violin 1 part), extending it from m. 386 to 390 (four and a quarter measures), then beginning the long descent at 390 and moving to the end of the movement at 399 (one measure shorter than in the final version; ex. 2b). And then, still dissatisfied, he discovered the true ending. In the final rewriting, the high C is held for five and a quarter measures, followed by the same descent in violin 1,

Ex. 2a. First version of violin 1 part, mm. 386–393, in autograph manuscript.

Ex. 2b. Second version of violin 1 part, mm. 386–399, in autograph manuscript.

with the lower parts added in full. Surely the tenuto markings in the violin 1 part at mm. 392 and 393, on each arrival at C, suggest Beethoven's awareness of the significance of each descending octave scale as a motivic and formal component within this passage—and indeed within the whole movement.

CONVERSATION

JS: Joel Smirnoff (violin 1); RC: Ronald Copes (violin 2); SR: Samuel Rhodes (viola); JK: Joel Krosnick (cello); LL: Lewis Lockwood

LL Let's begin with the opening character, the expressive world that you get into at the beginning of this movement.

SR After Haydn's opus 20 no. 2, are there any major quartets up to this time that begin with a cello solo?

JK But this is a cello solo in the lower register, with the left hand if you were playing on a keyboard. Whereas in Haydn you're below me—the cello is above middle C. In this quartet the cello isn't the top line. We discussed the opening of 18 no. 1, the kinetic energy of the motif, but this is a *melody,* a big melody stated twice at the opening of the piece. Also, it says in my program "Quartet in F major," but it sure is a while before you could prove that by me. It's very vague in terms of the triad— you have an A and a C, but that's all you have.

SR That's why bar 19 is so important, and the dolce at bar 30.

JS The so-called ostinato, or motor rhythm, has the slowest harmonic rhythm in history, basically. You have one tonic chord that lasts forever and then you have one dominant chord that lasts *really* forever. The idea of massive tensions that last forever predates the idea of the violin concerto opening cadenza, over a dominant chord, which is two opus numbers later. The piece begins rather bucolically but then builds to an incredible release of tension right away, and a very positive one: not a negative one but one that is very hopeful and—

SR Triumphant.

JS Triumphant, exactly. And that's a huge event and somehow that event is much bigger than anything you will encounter in any of the opus 18 quartets.

JK Maybe it's a bucolic opening in some sense, but there is still tension underneath. The accompanying parts could just hold the chord, but they're not holding the chord [*sings eighth-note rhythm*].

SR Here is the difficulty, the balance. First of all you have Beethoven's tempo, which is 88 to the half-bar, that's quite fast. If you were to follow that exactly you would find it's very hard to keep the expressive character going; it gets very tense. To balance the expressive character with the tension of the repeated notes in the accompaniment and the feeling of pulse and movement is not an easy thing. We certainly have problems both in realizing it and also in agreeing on what that should be in this movement.

JK Following Joel's comment about a level of tension emotionally, and speaking as somebody who plays this tune: as slow a harmonic rhythm as it is, to play a tune where—sing sweetheart, sing it—it says dolce, but [*sings melody and beats rhythm of accompaniment*]. That's quite some level of tension. It's terribly important that the chords are either incomplete or in irresolute position. So it's not only tense rhythmically, it's tense harmonically because you're waiting for the other shoe to drop.

LL There is certainly an element of harmonic ambiguity; the piece is poised in a semi-ambiguous state from the beginning.

JK Which really does affect the sound. We talk about teaching, for example: ah, it's a cello solo, a famous cello solo [*sings very broadly*]. But it's not that, because of the two elements we're talking about. And the first indication that it's an F major quartet, the three bars before the fortissimo [mm. 16–18] drop down into the low notes in the cello: G, C, C octave, and then F. A very important occurrence along with the first violin whole-notes.

LL Many wonderful things are packed into the first 20 measures or so, such as leading up to the first climactic four-octave span at bar 19—which is a trope on the opening of opus 18 no. 1, by the way—and the rise from one octave to multiple octaves.

JK But this moment [*sings m. 20*], transition though it may be, un-stable though it may be, if you don't play this the proper way, your fugue, about three minutes hence, doesn't make any sense—if you don't somehow manage a short-short-long artic-ulation.

JS One thing that's difficult is that subito piano in bar 8 for the three lower voices, because here you have a crescendo to a subito piano, but one has to respect the natural quality of the motor rhythm. So really there's a limit to what one can do and at the same time one doesn't want to get in the way of the singing of the *Hauptstimme,* which is the cello.

JK But at the same time, if you look at the cello part, it's mezzo-forte crescendo to piano. You know it's often practiced [*sings with hesitation at change of dynamic*], but it still is a line.

LL That's a change, by the way. The piano dynamic was originally one measure later [m. 9].

SR Where the first violin comes in.

LL It's one of those late changes.

JK But that's an enormous change. What, is there a penultimate version of this in the manuscript?

LL The piano dynamic was originally in ink in the next measure, but crossed out and added in red pencil in this one.

JS For me, one of the qualities about the opening which I find fascinating is there is at once a sense of excitement but also a sense of patience. There's a sense of a shimmering quality that stays very happily within one place, both on the tonic chord and then on the 4-3 chord for a very long time. And one patiently waits for something wonderful, and that patient quality is very much part of the experience of playing these openings; you want to wait and plan the end of the crescendo, as when one will eventually in Wagner when a crescendo goes for twenty bars.

JK Speaking to the sense of patience, I count four bars as one bar. I mean, harmonically one would count it that way.

JS The phrase is a very long question. There are many pieces that begin with a very short question, in other words, a phrase that ends on V: for example, the *Tragic Overture* of Brahms and Beethoven's opus 59 no. 2—which are basically the same thing: they just go I–V, two chords—or the Schubert "Unfinished" Symphony with its portentous unison. Basically these movements ask a question, a very portentous question, to which the rest of the movement will be an answer. But here's an eight-bar phrase where the last, the eighth, bar goes to the dominant and in a way that asks the question that will then be answered—of course, that eighth bar being a subito piano. [*laughter*]

RC But you were saying that he moved the piano marking in all three parts?

LL Yes. The facsimile of the autograph score has been published.

SR He didn't want the cello to go directly to the first violin.

LL Originally, yes, but he changed it later.

RC He was trying, I think, to avoid a squareness to that periodic structure.

LL Yes. But the squareness is more apparent than real. In measure 5, the cello starts the phrase again, but not on a consonant member of the tonic triad. It's starting on the sixth scale degree while the second violin and viola are continuing to play A and C, so that second member of the large phrase has a dissonant opening that the first doesn't have.

JK In our annotated score, I start the fifth bar on an up-bow rather than a down-bow and not only that but another way of avoiding squareness is the slur from bar 3 to 4.

SR Which is not repeated in the second phrase in that pattern [mm. 7–8].

LL No, it's not, but he needs to establish a motif. There are at least three important motives in the first four measures, every one of which has a life of its own.

RC He didn't change the articulation when he changed the piano?

LL No, he just moved the dynamic mark back a measure.

JK I don't think we put it in the annotated edition, but I doubt that my dynamic is as strong in the fifth bar as it is in the first bar, because of what you just mentioned.

SR We did put a dash on the D-natural of the first beat, an up-bow and a dash.

LL Of course, everything changes when instead of falling a fourth as it did the first time, it goes down one step to the first scale degree, so it starts a new mode of melodic motion.

JS Another thing: as he gets close to the fortissimo he adds double-stops so that the big V chord, più forte, is actually an eight-part chord. One thing we should say about performance in a quartet or any chamber music situation: when you play a double-stop, where it's implied that the composer really wishes he had another voice, you have to play big enough to sound like two voices. It's not enough to just play the same dynamic. You have to play more.

SR Here it's clearly enhancing that by pulling out all the stops, in a way.

LL And it's enhanced also by the first violin restating the original motive, but now in a tremendous augmentation to make the cadence [mm. 16–19]. You don't have to be an analytic fiend to believe this, it's too clear.

JK Over the last three bars of that, the cello drops an octave and a half, a huge drop, as the first violin goes up.

LL It makes the registral climax total, and coincides with the dynamic.

SR That's the hallmark for the middle-period quartets right there:

everything is expanded beyond the point that anyone could conceive.

LL Now, when you approach performance, or are coaching students about how to play this, do you try to include a sense of an aesthetic difference from the earlier phase, let's say, opus 18?

SR, RC, JS Definitely.

JK There really is a difference. One of the things that we'll get to in this piece as we go through is the arrivals—there's a major arrival in the F major material in bar 30, for example. What I'm getting at is there are in-betweens, and there are arrivals. And terribly important in this long a style is a different feeling of sound, vibrato, rhythmic instability for something like [*sings the motif in mm. 20–21*]. That's in-between. I think that one of the things that happens with even good young groups is that they want to play expressively all the time, all the way through. Well, this is a long time. If you play expressively the same way all the way through, then you indeed haven't moved anywhere.

RC It's a bit like reading a poem, or telling a story: if you use a consistent inflection to the voice regardless of what the words are, you lose the expressiveness.

JK Regardless of a side anecdote or a digression . . . For example, the dolce quality at bar 30 is tremendously important. Finally, okay, this is the home key for the first time, with a bass note, wow. Beethoven's own articulations, starting in bar 19, are very important, in terms of slurring across bar lines and the subito piano in 21. It's very unstable writing—to try to indicate terribly important material, to say don't sit down here, please. And when we do sit down in bar 30, a formidably different texture in F major with parallel thirds above it, and a complete triad, very rich, double-stops in the viola, sixths even.

JS   One really enters in a way into what could be called the Romantic style. At this point we're no longer walking this tightrope, as we said in opus 18. And in a way for the kids in our school, who are used to playing in a Romantic style—a lot of the time that's why they took up the instrument anyway, because they are romantic—this is a much easier style for them than the opus 18s. They are much more fish-in-water in this place than they are understanding the dual quality of the style of the 18s, so it's a little more natural for them. You know, here's the beginning of movie-length music [*laughter*]—really, where there is no way you can program this piece as a trifle. It becomes the evening's focus.

LL   The classical statement is that this is where the quartet becomes symphonic, which is a kind of cliché—but there's a point to it.

JS   And so the challenge for the performer, of course, becomes making sure that the listeners know where they are in this music at all times—especially when you have a piece like this one, where the exposition and the recap are not that long but the development is a monster. It's become a Frankenstein, you know, very quickly.

SR Like the *Eroica* Symphony, of course.

JS Same thing—where you get the new melody from the oboe in the *Eroica* Symphony as you get new things in this. So the challenge becomes different: for both the performer and the listener, it demands a different kind of concentration and a kind of planning that one didn't have to do before. It's like you're going on a big mountain trip and you've got to pack.

SR And not get lost.

JS Make sure you have the compass.

JK For example, again this comes up in teaching: between 48 and the second theme in 60 is something that is brilliant, important, and in-between. It's not that you play [*sings mm. 48ff in emphatic style*], tempted as you might be—it's a nice cello solo. But that's not what it's about. And again, as romantic as the kids are here, you need the idea of an intelligent romanticism, where if it's a movie-length score not every single thing you play is a love scene.

JS I meant "romantic" in the sense of heightened tension and emotions, whether it's violence, love, hatred—where everything is on the edge.

LL And everything is on a very large scale now, so the contrasts have to be on a large scale too.

JS Exactly. If you look at the idea of sforzando and fortissimo, it's clear that we're not at court anymore, because that contrast would be pretty unacceptable.

JK You know the famous anecdote that the cellist Romberg was playing the opening of the second movement of this and threw it on the floor and trampled on it.

LL There was also the violinist who was brought in to finger the first violin part. He said, "This is not music." And Beethoven is said to have replied: "This is not for you, it's for a later age."

JS Well, that's a big statement. It's what we were talking about before, the sense of marking the music so that it will be playable by another age, writing with that in mind.

LL It has an apocalyptic character. The whole conception is out of our world and looking forward to later times, in a progressive sense.

At some point, I have to get you to talk about the famous mystifying half-notes high and low [beginning in mm. 85, 144, and 332].

JK One of the things about this place [m. 85], these half-notes, is that harmonically it's very unstable: incomplete thirds, diminished sevenths, seventh chords, and all of it, so whatever one does, there's a moment of harmonic uncertainty and a sudden sense of "Where am I?" When you get to 91, V–I, and we're in the dominant. Some students play this very clearly, very determinedly, but without a feeling of mystery. The mystery is in the incompletion, in thirds, in sevenths, in diminished sevenths—the harmonic language is mysterious. You were quite clearly at the dominant before you did that. And then all of a sudden, oh dear, what? There is some quality of—

SR Suspension. And it's only when he gently sets you down on the other side—

JK We wrote in our edition "sotto voce, poco vibrato." We didn't write "slower," but if you are going to appear to be uncertain, you can't sound like the metronome is on.

SR Well, he slows you down anyway. It's not that you purposely slow it down, but if you just react—there is a tremendous crescendo, fortissimo, almost a crescendo to the end [of m. 84]— you have to take time. That's one of the places we wrote in a comma.

LL Before you attack the first high pair [m. 85].

SR So maybe there is a little more time than usual than in other places, to set that off. And then, although you feel the pulse continuing, because of the material it doesn't continue at such an agitated rate. It's a little bit calm there for a moment.

JK It is in groups of two bars and not in single bars.

LL That's right. He's alternating between dominant of D minor and dominant of C, twice. The second time the thing comes back in the development [m. 144], it's not six measures but eight measures long—

SR He brings it down by a sequence.

LL With diminished sevenths introduced that further complicate the harmonic implications.

JK But it is always taking something that might otherwise be clear and saying, "Ah, were you sure?"

JK Again, one would not say to somebody doing this: "Take time here." Sam just said something about a suspended impulse— getting people to realize that something is happening here, that they can't just go through and play. But you wouldn't say "Take time."

RC Frequently, a useful concept, especially working with students, is to talk about the difference between certainty and uncertainty and how certain things feel very comfortable harmonically. Beethoven, in particular, uses this juxtaposition of certainty and uncertainty as a very potent expressive device, and this is a great illustration of that, where he goes from an almost static certainty to something utterly uncertain.

LL As complicated as everything else is, it feels reasonably clear emotionally until you get to these passages. And then something very strange comes over it, so they occupy a space of their own, a strangeness.

JS This is a tremendously modern moment. It's a very forward-looking moment: you get to composers, especially when you get to serial music, who really feel that a single note is a big deal, a big event, and so you have a single note here, and a single note here, and a single note here. I've always had an objection, actually, to the idea that a single note is a big event. But the point is that here you have separated out a seemingly discontinuous series of notes and that is a very modern idea—in terms of a fragmentation.

SR If you look at the score of Webern, opus 28, the first movement, it looks exactly like that.

JS Exactly.

RC This becomes *Klangfarben*.

JS You get *Klangfarben* eventually, but you know it really is a very modern attempt—

LL Absolutely. The association of certain pitches with particular registers in which they occur is crucial.

JS With the buildup to that [m. 85], it gets so frenetic that in a way he gets to a point where he has to break the tension—where is he going to go from the two bars preceding it? He's dazed in a way from this madness, and then he is able to gather himself together and make a cadence, after that. And that's kind of how I see it.

LL This music was for a later age, after all.

JS Oh, yeah.

SR No question about it.

JK And even the forte at 89, all you can do is describe something. As compared to the fortissimo we got to, this is forte and the harmonic language is still "Where are we?" and then a moment later you do know. But even that forte is played with a different sort of sound quality, it's not solid and thick, it's still a little bow speed, still a little air, and an air of uncertainty. And then all of a sudden a moment later in 91, piano-dolce. Oh, do you understand where we were? And then the implications of the low C in the cello . . .

RC Harmonically at rest.

LL Settling back down again, but still with a memory of the strangeness in the air.

RC That's the wonderful thing about certainty: it does not have a particular emotional or dramatic connotation. The transition from uncertainty to certainty is usually not a sharp release. It can be really quite magical, as this is.

JK And to follow what Ron is saying, not therefore to say, "Play slower here. Take time." Again "take time" is a difficult thing.

RC Dangerous.

LL I have always loved that right after that, at measure 94 [1st violin part], innocuously there comes out of somewhere a figure that's going to have a life of its own. It's buried in the texture here but it's going to play an enormous role in the development section. So he's interweaving subtleties at a very high level of complexity.

JS And Brahms of course will take that and run with it.

JK Again, terribly important when one is teaching is to point out that it's not just down up-up, down up-up—don't say that so cavalierly. A moment later in that fugue you'd better have recognized this guy.

JS I would say that bar 94 is a variation of the measure two bars previous. And the point is that when you play a variation of something you want to play it as though you are ornamenting, being inventive, creating, improvising. That sense of spontaneous spark should give the listener something to think about.

SR He's recalling the very beginning of the piece and the motives there. They're all related to that.

LL It harkens back to several stages of transformation; and then at measure 107, where the cello seemingly has returned to the beginning but is really going on—

SR the false return—

LL that's the figure that moves on to the G-flat.

JK Now in terms of tempo-character, often we've had a problem at this moment of 103 to get back to the character and motion of the beginning and not to be under it.

LL Do you do something to prepare for the return of the theme, or do you just let it flow right into it?

SR We let it flow gradually from 97.

JK Yeah, but we put some forward arrows in there between 97 and 103. That's not to push it, but . . .

LL I'm thinking really of how 102 gets to 103.

JK It's what Sam is saying. It's already from the cello's playing in 97. Then Joel takes me up on it, and Ron . . .

RC One of the things that's very tricky about this, of course, is there is a subito piano marked at 103 in the inner voices here, but the crescendo that the cello has goes into the mezzo forte. So there's very little real sense of a subito piano as an event; it's more of a pragmatic marking, telling us our roles.

JK This place that we play into the subito piano in 97 was one of the places we wrote a comma with a slash.

JK Because it can't stop completely.

SR It doesn't go straight ahead, it goes back a little bit. From there on we use that moment to pull us gradually toward the tempo at 103. And we're back at the first tempo.

JK At that moment when you ask what happens at 102, it either has happened by then or it's too late.

SR It goes straight ahead through that bar.

JK Especially for the cello, who doesn't have a subito piano on the end of that crescendo.

SR Of course, you don't want to set up that return as a real one; it just sort of appears and goes on. You think you're back at the beginning but it goes on.

LL By the way, in the work of those music historians who used to talk about sonata form as the be-all and end-all, this is the landmark piece in which there is no repeat sign for the exposition.

SR Is this the first instance?

LL Just about. It's a landmark for it.

JS In other words, the first false return.

SR The first important one.

LL Important in view of the formal height of the string quartet as a genre. If you think of the quartet world—and Beethoven always thinks inside genres anyway—he's got Haydn F major, Mozart F major, everything behind him, all pounding in his head. It's a moment when something is saying, "This is where I have changed the whole language of the genre."

How about a little bit about how the recapitulation works? If you could tell me where it is that would be particularly wonderful. [*laughter*]

SR It would be.

JK You want everything, huh?

SR In one sense, it's in 242.

LL Right, but it's not. That's a I-6 chord, and it's the wrong figure.

SR In another sense, it's 254.

JK I remember once I was with Leonard Stein, my late dear friend on the West Coast; he was an assistant to Schoenberg among other things. I was working on a contemporary solo piece, a very fine piece and all that, and I was practicing it in his house. Come the recap with all kinds of re-registrations, and everything is in the same order it was the first time, and Leonard said, "You know, everything's in the same order it was the first time. What's the fun in that?" [*laughter*] —Which is what Schoenberg would have said, and certainly was what Beethoven did here. The material is absolutely memorable, absolutely recognizable, has tremendous character—you don't have to say it the same way you said it the first time.

LL It also allows him to expand in a completely new way when the first theme finally does come back, and move out into different harmonic areas than he's been in before, toward D-flat.

JK You asked something about this moment, the bar before the recap itself—the second bar of that fortissimo [m. 253]. That's a tremendous moment because, just by dropping two octaves, the cello has done what we've been talking about all along: added to the fortissimo by suddenly doubling the register.

LL While the first violin comes down two octaves to the same pitch, C [mm. 254–255], as if it was not quite perfectly synchronized thematically, which is another beautiful mixture.

JK We haven't talked at all about the quality of the extended development in terms of the fugato. Because this is an unprecedented moment, bar 185—this is really a symphonic moment.

SR This is the first pianissimo in the piece. It exists on a dimension below everything that has occurred up to that time.

JK And then with a polyphonic gathering of all kinds of things, written sempre pianissimo. And the materials are not necessarily the major materials of the piece. And again in teaching that: I remember a very good group playing this, and stopping them and saying, "What are these materials?" They didn't know, and I said, "Wait a minute, you need to find them." I use this often in teaching: when you're playing a development section, you look back and you may find you didn't say something you needed to say in the exposition. Or in this case, in the beginning of the development. This whole fugato, doubling the size of the development section, is extraordinary, *Eroica*-like—it's huge. From the very beginning harmonically it was at least in one to the bar, if not in two bars, and you better have the tempo together; otherwise this fugue just sits there. It's very long.

SR Also keeping three out of the four entrances as soft as possible. The fourth one [cello in m. 198] starts in that way and then very suddenly changes the texture to just the opposite.

RC It's a very quick crescendo [mm. 201–202].

JK A two-bar crescendo to forte after 16 bars of pianissimo.

JS What that implies is that there is tension latent throughout the whole of that fugato which only erupts in those two bars. In terms of playing the thing, it's not just that one plays pianissimo, but it's pianissimo with a terrible sense of dread of these two bars which enter the key of F minor.

JK We focus the sound, we don't vibrate—

JS It's not that it's spaced out, it's greatly motivated.

JK Pianissimo does not mean relaxation in either tempo or articulation.

RC Most of the time that's true. Very frequently pianissimos imply something that has more tension. Again it comes from the specialness of it as a dynamic, the pronounced softness.

JK It's not piano, it's pianissimo.

RC Right. The same theme is often forte.

SR One of these themes is very recognizable, it's been there all the time. The other one is kind of recognizable but it's never been quite formulated in that way.

LL   May I make another suggestion? This piece is absolutely for the future and is as progressive in all its conception as you could ask for, but a first movement in F major which has room for a fugato in the development is 18/1 again. That happens in quartets, but not in piano sonatas. It can happen in symphonies but he hasn't done it yet, except in the *Eroica*. It's part of the sense of the largeness of purpose of the genre now that has room for everything, including the most serious discourse of counterpoint.

JS   The sound that one has to use for all of this tension building in the fugato eventually creates a kind of harmonic train wreck, where the piece more or less breaks down in 210. It's at a very high dynamic and it's very hard to tell harmonically where it's going to land, because it's a diminished seventh. The sound of that particular moment, those sforzandi in forte, or really fortissimo—that's a new sound that hasn't quite happened yet. That's really a frontier.

LL   It gradually starts coming down in intensity.

JS   And that very peculiar chord, with a suspension.

RC   But you get the feeling that he is culminating in something. It's that there's no way out from this. There's the sense that it's growing and growing, and he just turns the corner.

JS   Well, there is a tragic quality to it.

JS It's a very beautiful moment and big. And that's really a new event right there.

JK After all of that one cannot stop—the language is dreadful, filled with dread.

LL It turns out you're heading toward the dominant, which might feel like it's going to start preparing for an eventual return, but it's still going to be quite a while before it decides to do it.

SR He may still go to another extreme.

LL There is always more time for more things to happen in this movement.

JS That's right, but that goes back to the idea of patience—that one is finding one's way as he was finding his way. The piece itself maybe is describing his own sense of composing it.

LL Which we would love to know more about. There are very, very few sketches, and nothing for this movement. They got lost and what there is for the other movements hasn't really been worked on, but the autograph is very rich.

SR Skipping ahead a little bit through the recapitulation to the coda and the massive statement of the main theme in fortissimo sforzandos with the quartet spread out as far as it will go [mm. 348ff]. It's the culmination of that very first crescendo in the piece, of the first theme, finally reaching its goal. It's one of those places that almost transcends the string quartet. You have to try to get more from the group than it was intended to give.

JK And 347 is again a tremendous moment where this intensity spreads out, two octaves in the cello.

SR We put a wavy line with a backward arrow through that bar.

LL What does the backward arrow mean?

SR It means that you are slowing down, I guess. Maybe just a wavy line is enough.

JK We wrote dashes over those sforzandi, because again sforzandi can be numbers of things; we feel this adds to the fortissimo. The fortissimo is also legato.

RC Let me also say something about that squiggly line in the measure before, in the fortissimo [m. 347]. It's a great illustration of how it's not really simply a question of taking time, but of feeling difficulty—because there's also a tremendous momentum, a feeling of wanting to go through that measure along with something to resist it. This is the kind of conversation that we frequently had when we were talking about what notations to use. There is no notation that can get that; what we came up with implies that something is going on here with the flow of time.

SR If you want to prepare that next moment the way it should be, you have to pay attention to this.

JK And also there's a più forte in 346, but don't tell me that the cello does a two-octave drop without getting louder. [*laughter*] So there's no crescendo, but he wrote it.

JS Of course.

SR It's gathering.

LL I have something I have to ask you about. For years, I've been saying that 348 is the climactic moment, because you finally have the theme in the first violin over full root support and it's absolutely planted. Sure enough, after five measures in comes this dominant of the dominant, that B natural, that cuts the legs out from under it. That's the feeling. Can you help me understand that better?

JS Why is there a G-6-5 chord in measure 352? All it really is: he is trying to raise the tension and he's doing it by raising the bass line. The bass line goes up in steps and he could have gone to a B-flat—he wants to get to his C pedal-tone, right? So the question is: is he going to write a B-flat or a B-natural?

LL It isn't that I'm questioning that it's the right note. It's one of the ultimate cases of having finally arrived and yet you find out, oh no, there's another 40 yards to go to the summit even though I'm out of oxygen.

JS That's right, that's the idea. It suggests even more tension.

LL I'm going to wring you out more.

JS Always more.

SR But it's not only the strong aspect of the theme that is realized here; it's also the dolce aspect of the theme, which he still has to do, and he has to create space to realize that later.

LL Yes, and there is still a coda to come.

SR Finally he lets that make the piece disappear, and puts an end on it.

LL By the way, I have doped out from the autograph three different variants to the ending. He didn't originally sustain that high C in the first violin for all those measures [mm. 386–390]; instead it starts coming down early. He doesn't like that, changes it again.

JS That's interesting about the C because the idea of sustaining a note like that really goes against what was instrumentally possible, especially with the bow, the pre-Tourte bow—because it just didn't want to play a pedal tone that high for that long. Like many other great composers, including Bach of course, he makes the instrumentalists expand their technique in order to reflect what the composer is trying to describe.

LL And doesn't it also beautifully pick up what happened in 254 at the recap moment, when you were doing it an octave lower and now you get to do it in the three-octave way that is so characteristic for this enormously expanded style.

JS One thing that we should point out about the string quartet is that string instruments have a huge range in terms of pitch—all of them—and that enables Beethoven to develop a language in which he will utilize every aspect from top to bottom of the instrument; that will become part of how he's going to create breadth in the sound, in something like the scherzo of opus

131 between the second violin and viola, the idea of jumping intervals. One thing that I have been very aware of, and I talk about all the time with my students, is the difference between how Beethoven wrote for the strings in the orchestra and how he wrote for the quartet. There are only two instances where he writes the kind of sustained ostinato writing, motor writing, for the middle voices of a quartet that he does for the orchestra, and that's the end of the development of 18/4, first movement, and the development of the "Harp" quartet. But he will not ask the orchestra to do, ever, what he asks the quartet to do. It will not happen.

LL They weren't soloists. They weren't individual players of such quality. They're the guys in the section.

JS Wait a second, I used to be in an orchestra. [*laughter*]

LL Everyone here has.

RC I think it's very interesting, his use of the B-natural here: in 385 at the end of that same passage, he finishes with the B-natural again. Here it's just a passing tone but it's been prepared.

JS One thing that's quite lovely in terms of his resolving the movement: The first time, as you pointed out, that we ever heard [*sings motif from m. 94*], which was this little variation—it's how he closes the movement.

LL It's still around.

JS It's still around. In other words, he shows us [*sings the opening tune*] in 387 and [*sings the motif from m. 389*] and that's how he brings us in a way to this restful quality of F major which he tags the final cadence onto. It's a lovely memory. He reminds you how you got there.

LL What do you do about the tenutos on 392 and 393?

JS I think that's a defensive marking. I think he's saying don't hit these notes.

RC And don't play them short.

JS In other words, he wants a melodiousness. In the context of staccato, I think he's saying soften the attack. So that's how I interpret it.

JK It's also over a pedal that Sam and I are holding, so it's not a question of slowing down. That's one chord for five bars [mm. 391–395].

JS One more thing about this quartet: there is a lot of dividing into two teams in this piece, the boys and the girls [*laughter*]

JK Upper and lower.

RC We're talking about SATB.

JK You know this famous line in a lot of the serial composers: What's the difference in an octave transposition? When you go to a Mozart opera, there's fifteen years' or a possible gender difference in an octave.

JS In the Prussian quartets and the *concertante* style of Mozart, there's a kaleidoscopic quality to how the alliances in the quartet change. But in this piece there certainly is a division between upper two and lower two at many places. For instance, the horn intervals in the recap, in 279, where the higher voices have a duet and then the two boys answer [mm. 283ff]; and our modernist moment [m. 85]. There's a lot of that. I don't think it quite happened before, the idea of the division of the group into high and low in this particular way. One does feel when we play in horn intervals [mm. 30ff] that it could be two oboes, it could be two horns. There's something in the symphonic realm about this.

ANNOTATED SCORE

Opus 59 no. 1, first movement

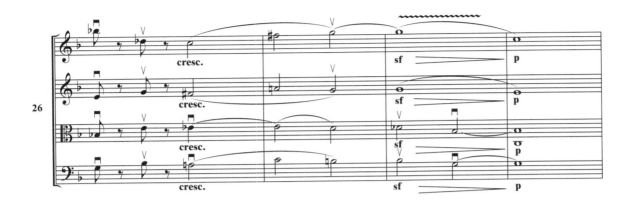

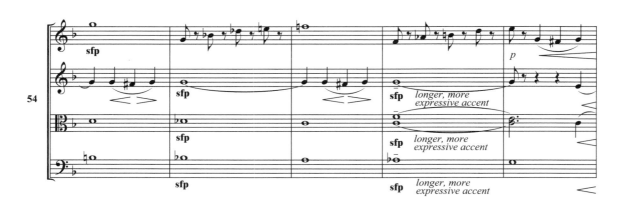

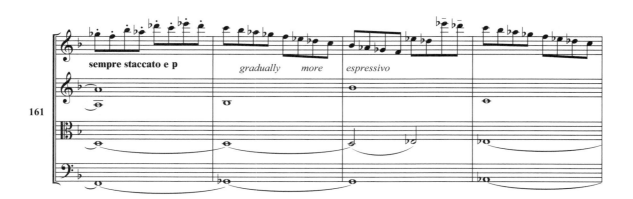

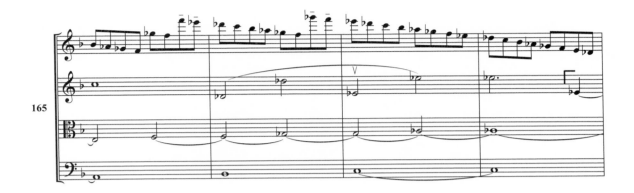

longer and longer articulations

cresc.

cresc.

cresc.

cresc.

pesante

*pochissimo
meno mosso*

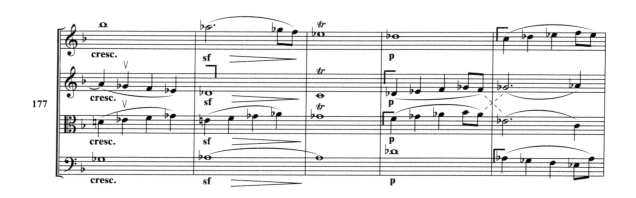

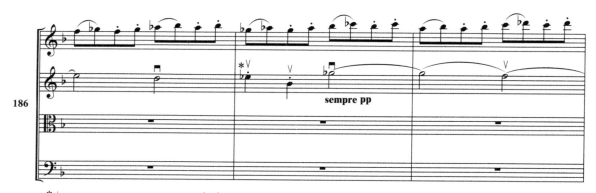

* ♩ *a bit longer and less lifted than* ♪ ♪ *of bar 20*

189

193

197

*♩ *a bit longer and less lifted than* ♪ ♩ ♪ *of bar 20*

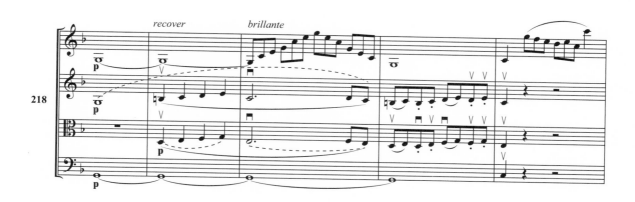

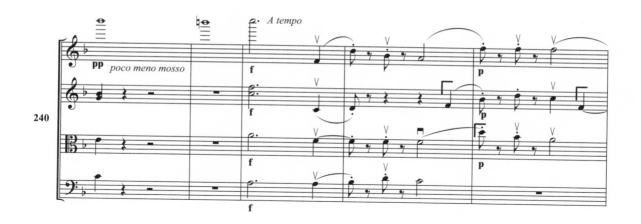

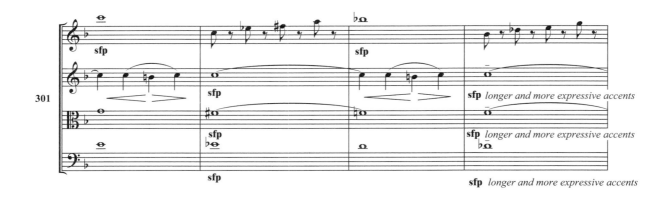

Opus 130

THE LATE QUARTETS

In 1822, about seventeen years after Count Razumovsky's commission, Prince Nikolai Galitzin, another Russian aristocrat, requested Beethoven to write "two or three new quartets, for which I would be pleased to pay you for your trouble what you judge appropriate."[1] Galitzin, an active cellist and a longtime Beethoven admirer, was a patron with some claim to serious musicianship. He played chamber music, gave recitals in cities across Russia, and made and published arrangements of Beethoven's works. A stay in Vienna in 1804–1806, when he was in his early twenties, had enabled him to hear the chamber music of Haydn, Mozart, and Beethoven, and he later described that visit as having left him "captivated by the heavenly harmonies which Beethoven generously bestowed on his early quartets and quintets."[2]

Beethoven's letters to Galitzin in the 1820s include his usual expressions of gratitude to a new patron, expectations about payment, and his promise to compose the new quartets. They also contain a few remarks about his aesthetic aims regarding these quartets, which from 1825 to his death in March 1827 were his sole creative preoccupation. As the months passed he thanked Galitzin not only for the commission but also for having been a subscriber to the *Missa Solemnis;* in fact, the Prince had a hand in promoting the first performance of the Mass in Saint Petersburg in April 1824. His reward was the dedication of Beethoven's *Consecration of the House* overture, op. 124, in 1825.

Immersed in the new quartets, Beethoven explained to the publisher Schott in March 1825 that "the violin quartets are still being composed . . . [and] the second one is almost finished."[3] He composed the E-flat quartet op. 127 early that year, then turned to the A minor quartet op. 132, which he finished by the summer. By the end of the year he had completed the trilogy with op. 130, the B-flat major quartet, with the Grosse Fuge as finale. The next two quartets—op. 131, in C-sharp minor, and op. 135, in F major, written without commission—were Beethoven's last works in any genre, and after op. 135 the new finale for op. 130 (written to replace the Grosse Fuge, which became op. 133) was his last completed movement. He left sketches for an unfinished C major string quintet at his death on 26 March 1827.

Beethoven's most interesting letter to Galitzin is one he wrote in July 1825, answering a query that the Prince had sent him concerning a musical detail in op. 127. Galitzin had reported that musicians in Saint Petersburg were troubled as to whether a certain note in the viola part of the slow movement of op. 127 was a D-flat or a C. Beethoven answered in painstaking detail, explaining why the note in question had to be D-flat for motivic, harmonic, and melodic reasons—"if I had written *c*, the melody would have been destroyed."[4] But as valuable as Beethoven's remarks about this textual question is what he tells Galitzin about his artistic outlook:

> Believe me when I say that my supreme aim is that my art should be welcomed by the noblest and most cultivated people. Unfortunately we are dragged down from the supernatural element in art only too rudely into the earthy and human sides of life. Yet is it not precisely they who are related to us? And without really wanting or being able to amass great riches, we must see to it that they in general shall bless our memory, seeing that, when all is said and done, we are not great Princes, who, as we know, merely leave the welfare of their subjects to the future and to God.[5]

The late quartets complete Beethoven's life-work. Although it is not easy to pinpoint the start of his last period, it lasted from about 1815 to his death in 1827. After the seventh and eighth symphonies (1812) and the revision of *Leonore* as *Fidelio* (1814), his creative output slowed significantly. The vast tide that had rolled on from the *Eroica* to the Eighth Symphony now receded. These years brought a few progressive efforts such as the piano sonata op. 90 (1814) and the song cycle *An die ferne Geliebte* (1815), but it was more a time of gathering his forces for a new resurgence.[6]

By 1815–1816, with the two cello sonatas op. 102 and the A major piano sonata op. 101, he had begun to reap the harvest of his patience. In these works a new poetic sensibility emerges that feels detached from the powerful strivings of his earlier music. Thereafter the "late style" poured forth in full glory with the "Hammerklavier"

Sonata (1818), by far the longest of his piano sonatas. From here the path broadened to the last piano sonatas, opp. 109, 110, and 111 (1819–1822), and the *Diabelli* Variations (1819–1822); the *Missa Solemnis,* planned for Archduke Rudolph's installation as Archbishop of Olmütz in 1820 but not finished until 1822; and the Ninth Symphony (1822–1824). The Ninth was his first symphony in more than ten years, its hybrid form combining powerful symphonic writing with his setting of Friedrich Schiller's *Ode to Joy* for vocal soloists and chorus. The Ninth aimed to revive public awareness of democratic ideals that were fading in the wake of the post-Napoleonic restoration. With *Fidelio,* it is Beethoven's most direct tribute to freedom in a politically darkening world.

His newly developing style accompanied the transformation of Beethoven's personal outlook during these years. Increasing deafness and social isolation left him a lonely and aging artist, alienated from the pleasure-loving musical world of Biedermeier Vienna. In 1812–1818 he kept a diary, in which he recorded excerpts from Homer and other classical writers, Kant and other moderns, and Masonic sayings. He also transcribed writings from Hindu and Brahman sources, including the *Bhagavad-Gita,* which resonated for him in their affirmation of inward spirituality and also reinforced his Masonic beliefs.[7]

From 1818 on, Beethoven's deafness reached the point at which conversation with him required the aid of "conversation books," small blank booklets in which visitors could write remarks and ask questions. The conversation books that survive, which form a valuable if one-sided record of what was said by visitors and friends during his last years, cover many subjects, including music, performers, politics, and personal matters. The nearly twelve dozen surviving conversation books extend from 1818 to early March 1827, just before his death.[8]

Beethoven's obsessive habits, those of a deaf, reclusive artist who was struggling to raise his adopted nephew while concentrating on his work, above all on the last quartets, drove him even further into himself and the world of his imagination. His diary and other evidence, including his copying into a conversation book in 1820 of a maxim from Kant, the most important philosopher of his early years, shows his striving to hold his life steady while he reached for the transcendental in his art: "the moral law within us and the starry sky above us—Kant!!!"[9] Beethoven believed in "freedom and progress" in art, as he told the Archduke, and although he maintained the inherited worldview of an Enlightenment intellectual, he embraced that part of the Romantic movement that focused on individual artistic sensibility.[10] As products of his own deeply personal "empire of the mind," the late quartets were too difficult for all but a few sympathetic contemporaries, and certainly so for the public and the critics; to many they seemed the obscure ruminations of a deaf and possibly mad artist. It took more than half a century before they began to gain the hallowed position they now occupy in the chamber music literature. And yet, as we can see nearly two hundred years later, these quartets are the natural outcome of Beethoven's lifetime development.

The intermingling of musical ideas in his sketches for the A minor and B-flat major quartets continues in his work on the next two, opp. 131 and 135, and is found to some extent in the finished works themselves. Their interconnections argue for an integrated conception behind all of them; they are like an extended family of highly profiled individuals who nevertheless have some features in common. Many analysts have noted the close intervallic relationship between the opening of op. 132 (7–1–6–5) and that of op. 131, as well as a parallel connection with the opening of the Grosse Fuge. And at least as important as motivic and thematic relationships are Beethoven's creation of a new quartet style, his experimentation with forms and proportions, and his challenges to tradition in ways that go beyond the iconoclasm of his earlier works.

How he does this is far from obvious, although the results have not been lost on performers or listeners. But even if we cannot pluck out the mystery, we can see some of his methods.

Formal innovation. New means of organization appear both within movements and in the larger shaping of each quartet. The first composed, op. 127, is still in the standard four movements, but sketches show that at one time Beethoven thought of making it a six-movement composition. Anomalies abound throughout the work, and its first movement deviates markedly from even his most adventurous earlier procedures, in its three statements of the Maestoso that opens the movement and in its concealment of the moment of recapitulation.

In the later quartets we find further deviations from traditional norms. Opus 132 has five movements; op. 130 has six, with the Grosse Fuge as the original finale; op. 131 has seven numbered movements (so numbered in the first edition), although its transition movement no. 3 is only eleven measures long. Indeed, op. 131 is altogether a formal anomaly. Finally, although op. 135 reverts to the traditional four-movement pattern, its finale, beginning with a slow introduction marked *Grave,* dramatically transforms the *Grave* when it returns later in the movement.

As Beethoven reshapes inherited formal procedures, these works embody implicit critiques of the very forms they employ. The first movements of opp. 127, 132, 130, and 135, the Allegro second movement of op. 131, the finales of opp. 127, 131, and 135, and the "little" finale to op. 130 have a nominal relationship to the traditional sonata forms that Beethoven had inherited and exploited throughout his earlier career; but their musical ideas overwhelm formal issues and render them far less meaningful. For example, it is hard to determine whether the first movement of op. 132 has two expositions or two recapitulations. And in the variation slow movements of four out of the five works—opp. 127, 132, 131, and 135—Beethoven now goes far beyond the classical model that uses successive rhythmic diminutions leading to a slow variation before the final one. Now the larger formal structure is conditioned by an overarching unfolding of the movement from its initial theme through its successive elaborations in strikingly different emotional and expressive contexts. The process typically reaches a series of climactic points, then concludes with a quiet, lingering coda.

Fugue and variation. New means of integration emerge both in the development of musical ideas and in the many new sonorities that Beethoven devises in these quartets, for example the passage *sul ponticello* in the Scherzo of op. 131. New too is the predominance in these works of fugue and variation, with sonata-form movements less central than before. It's true that Beethoven had been writing variation movements since childhood, and that he had composed his share of fugal or fugato movements, as in the finale of op. 59 no. 3. But in the late quartets the variation slow movements are expanded freely, and the fugal movements—above all the first movement of op. 131 and the

Grosse Fuge as finale of op. 130—are conceived with a freedom and depth that could not have been found in the string quartets before them. Along with the finale of the "Hammerklavier" Sonata and of the A-flat major sonata op. 110, they embody the late Beethoven's desire to meet Bach on fully equal terms and to show, as he once put it, that the language of fugue could be rendered poetic. At the same time, while formal procedures are often far more complex than in his earlier works, he can sometimes maintain the sense that more traditional gestures still organize phrases and climaxes—though these passages are now presented in elliptical and mysterious ways.

Titles and mottos. Verbal headings for certain movements suggest the expressive qualities for which Beethoven is striving in these works, whether personal, as in the slow movement of op. 132, designated "Holy Song of Thanksgiving to the Divinity by a Convalescent, in the Lydian mode," with its contrasting passages in pure D major marked "Feeling new strength"; or abstract, as in the enigmatic, gesturally embodied question and answer that ends op. 135: "Muss es sein? Es muss sein!" As elsewhere in Beethoven's late work (above all in the bass recitatives in the Ninth Symphony) there is the sense that he is reaching the borders of what instrumental music can express.

Crossing of genres. The most overt example of Beethoven's borrowing of movement-genres from other domains is the Cavatina of op. 130. A cavatina is a contemplative opera aria traditionally used in *opera seria.* Such an aria often follows a slow tempo with a faster concluding one, and sometimes appears just before a finale—as the op. 130 Cavatina does.

Voice-leading. When Karl Holz, the second violinist of the

Schuppanzigh Quartet in these years, asked Beethoven about the late quartets, the composer replied with some revealing general remarks, saying among other things that in these works he had devised a "new kind of voice-leading."[11] Beethoven was well aware of the complexity of part-writing in these compositions: their use of registral extremes in new ways; the resolution of dissonances in registers other than those in which they are introduced; the intensification of the linear integrity of every instrumental part within the larger texture; and the extreme density of the quartet sonorities, whether they are overtly contrapuntal or employ more traditional dialogue textures. Although these quartets are written for four instruments, suggestions of other voices briefly appear, coalesce, intertwine, dissolve, and reappear. Even in the Cavatina, in which the first violin is the "singing" part, all parts in fact have singing roles, and the violin 1 is best understood as first among equals. This principle, enlarged and applied in infinitely complex ways, governs the late quartets.

∞

Beethoven's experimental approach to quartet writing in these works helps explain the special history of the quartet in B-flat major, op. 130, the third of the Galitzin series, whose form is unlike that of any other Beethoven work. The original movement-plan called for a fairly normal-sized though very dense first movement in a type of sonata form, followed by four short movements of very diverse styles and categories: a highly compressed Scherzo in B-flat minor, virtually a bagatelle; a D-flat major Andante con moto; an Alla danza tedesca, i.e., a waltz, in

G major (originally conceived in A major for op. 132); a heartfelt Cavatina in E-flat major, Adagio molto espressivo; and an immense fugal finale, "tantôt libre, tantôt recherchée" ("partly free, partly strict"), which became known as the Grosse Fuge. This was later replaced by a lighter Allegro finale in B-flat major, 2/4.

Unlike the other late quartets, op. 130 has no variation movement, no long Scherzo, no long slow movement (the third movement is a subtle Andante in "walking" tempo rather than a probing slow movement). The proportions of the quartet in its original form are unlike any other Beethoven work—but the big radical feature is the enormous fugal finale, which dwarfs the earlier movements while it also integrates them.

The work was first performed on 21 March 1826 with the Grosse Fuge as finale, to mixed response. Audiences liked the inner movements, especially the Alla danza tedesca and the Cavatina, but were baffled by the fugue, which the critics found incomprehensible—"like Chinese."[12] Beethoven was soon persuaded by his publisher Artaria and Karl Holz to separate the fugue from the rest of the work and write a more accessible finale for the quartet. The Grosse Fuge was published separately as op. 133. Though critical debate has raged over whether the Grosse Fuge or the "little" finale is the proper conclusion for the quartet, no choice between them is necessary except in performance. With the fugue, the work becomes an end-oriented cycle with the finale as the goal; with the second finale, the six movements attain a more balanced equilibrium, and the last movement, while it stands up to its predecessors, lightens the final impression of the work with its grace and ease.

THE FIRST MOVEMENT

A familiar image of Beethoven in his last years shows him tramping the streets of Vienna with a sheaf of music paper in his coat pocket on which he could write down ideas as they came to him. From the early summer of 1825 pocket sketch-leaves survive that yield important clues to the origins of op. 130. These pencil jottings were followed by more developed sketches that he made in the desk-sketchbook that came to be called "De Roda" (after a Spanish collector, Cecilio de Roda).[1] This book contains sketches for the first five movements of op. 130, in their final order.

Although the full array of precompositional material for op. 130 has yet to be thoroughly studied, enough has been discovered to permit a provisional glimpse of Beethoven's earliest ideas for this quartet.[2] Especially suggestive is this preliminary entry in the De Roda sketchbook: "letztes Quartett mit einer ernsthaften und schwergängigen Einleitung" ("the last quartet with a serious and heavy-going introduction").[3] "Last" here means the third quartet of the Galitzin commission; in Beethoven's characterization of the planned introduction as "serious" and "heavy-going" we recognize op. 130. This notation accords with two earlier sketch ideas for the quartet in the Moscow pocket sketchbook. There, an entry in C major marked "3tes Quartett" ("3rd quartet") is replaced on a later page by a new musical idea for the first Allegro, now in B-flat major and marked "mit Adagio vor" ("with an Adagio before it"). This second entry fixes the key of the work as B-flat major but it is still very far from the final version (ex. 1).

After settling on a basic character for the slow introduction, Beethoven turns to an array of concept sketches for his finale. One or two are in 6/8 meter and one is marked "Fugha" (ex. 2).[4] In a typical early stage of composition, Beethoven first determines the idea of the opening material even before he has its pitches and rhythms firmly in mind and then sweeps forward to think about the finale, framing the work by outlining its beginning and end. And it is surely important for the whole conception of the work that the final movement is to be some kind of fugue.

Ex. 1. Very early sketch for the opening Allegro (Moscow sketchbook, p. 25, st. 6–7, mm. 1–9). As transcribed by Vyaskova, the upbeat to m. 1 in the lower part is an eighth-note, while the upper part has a quarter-note. In this example, both are shown as eighth-notes.

letztes Stück des quartetts in B

Ex. 2. Two early sketch ideas for the finale, in B-flat major; the second is marked "Fugha" (De Roda sketchbook, fol. 14r).

Ex. 3. Sketch for the opening phrase, in full harmony (De Roda sketchbook, fol. 13v).

In a more advanced though still early sketch for the opening of the movement, Beethoven arrives at the basic thematic opening of the Adagio, whose shape will generate the movement and indeed the whole quartet, but he has apparently not yet settled on the following Allegro (ex. 3). Fixing the Adagio opening establishes one of the starkly contrasting musical ideas from which the movement will be built. When we compare the De Roda full sketch of the first four bars to the final version, new facets of the diamond appear.

Both the De Roda and the final versions of mm. 1–4 present the opening phrase as a pair of two-bar units with the familiar harmonic motion I–V, V–I (in the following discussion, I use "A1" for the first unit, from the opening to the second beat of m. 2, and "A2" for the second unit, the third beat of m. 2 to the second beat of m. 4). They also have the same upper line and the same primary harmonic content and voice-leading. In the final version Beethoven intensifies A1 by starting in piano dynamic, making a crescendo through the first full measure, and then suddenly falling back to piano for the arrival at m. 2; the same dynamics govern the phrase A2.

There are two big differences between the two versions, though: first, in the sketchbook, the first phrase is in four full voices throughout, whereas in the final version it is monophonic, beginning in unison in the upper strings and with the cello an octave lower for the first four notes before the phrase blossoms into harmony. The *misterioso,* ruminative quality of the phrase arises not only from its harmonic ambiguity but also from its odd rhythm and pacing, in which the first, apparently tonic, pitch is the upbeat and the ensuing descent from 7 begins on the downbeat.[5] The second difference is that in the sketch version the two phrases are at the same pitch level, but in the final version A1 begins restricted to one octave, then widens to a twelfth at the second beat of m. 2. The answering phrase A2 expands to two octaves, and is in full four-voice harmony. In other words, the original sketched idea of the opening phrase already contains its primary features, in pitch-content, rhythm, voice-leading, and basic expression—but in the final version Beethoven dramatically contrasts the two phrases in texture and octave-register.

In the final version, the opening figure is a monophonic four-note chromatic descent, B-flat—A—A-flat—G, that is open to various harmonic interpretations. It can be heard in B-flat major, E-flat major, or even in F major until the final eighth-note of m. 1, when it gains harmonic clarity with the four-note C minor harmony (II of B-flat major) that now locates the phrase in B-flat major. The upper line remains in unison during the chromatic descent, but expands to full harmony as it becomes diatonic.[6] Then the second phrase, with its ex-

pansion to two octaves, gains new breathing space as the violin 1 repeats the four-note chromatic descent with close support from the
lower strings (notably with a rising cello line from B-flat to F in
mm. 3–4) and closes the whole phrase with the cadential motion from
7 to 1 (A—B-flat), a two-note gesture that will play an important role
later in the movement. The completion of the next, larger phrase
(mm. 4–7) is articulated by the same steady upward motion in the violin 1 from B-flat to F (now through E-natural to inflect the arrival at the
F major harmony at m. 7), growing in intensity through the crescendo
and further expanding the registral span to three octaves at m. 7.

The introduction continues at mm. 7–8 with two new ideas that
contrast with one another and with the preceding material: first, the
linear progression F—F-sharp—G in the cello at 7–8 (thus producing
an upward chromatic motion from the dominant pitch, F, to its neighbor, G), designated "B" in this discussion; second, the gently falling
three-note figures of m. 8, a motif that will also play a role later.[7]

FORM OF THE MOVEMENT

If we now look at the larger formal strategy that shapes the first movement we can better evaluate its features and see how the surviving
sketches relate to the totality and the details.

Introduction and exposition

Mm. 1–14. Adagio, B-flat major, 3/4. Two contrasting segments, A1
+ A2 (mm. 1–7) and B (7–14), each with its own motivic content and
textures.

Mm. 14/4–19. Allegro, B-flat major, 4/4. Two new contrasting themes: C (violin 1, mm. 14/4ff, cascading downward through thirds, then returning upward, in groups of four sixteenth-notes; and D (violin 2, mm. 15–16), the four-note figure beginning on the second beat.

Mm. 20–24. Adagio, 3/4, return of the A segment. The opening Adagio returns in the dominant, with A1 in the cello in low register (20/3–22/2) and A2 in the viola in mid-register (22/3–24/2). This early return of the first Adagio segment calls into question whether the extended opening Adagio is really an introduction, or whether the exposition actually started from the very beginning with two alternating tempi—Adagio and Allegro—which then reappear at the end of the exposition. I prefer the latter analysis, as it sharpens our awareness that the entire exposition is built on their basic contrasts.

Precedents in Beethoven's earlier works for tempo contrasts that create larger formal shapes go as far back as the piano sonatas "Pathétique," op. 13, and the "Sonata quasi una fantasia," op. 27 no. 1; closer in genre and key is the finale of op. 18 no. 6, "La Malinconia."[8] In that quartet movement the long opening Adagio (44 mm.) also returns twice in abbreviated form (just ten measures of the Adagio reappear at mm. 195–209, followed soon by two measures of it at 210–211), both alternating with Allegretto material. But these returns of the Adagio occur about two-thirds of the way through the movement and are not heard again, as melancholy gives way to the joyous Allegretto that dominates the rest of the movement.

In op. 130 the interface between Adagio and Allegro is far more subtle. Melodic figures and harmonic details of the Adagio weave their way into the Allegro, yet the two principal sections remain so clearly demarcated by tempo and content that they can shape the entire movement and maintain their individuality. They are juxtaposed four times in the course of the movement: at the opening; at the moment when the exposition modulates to the dominant; at the juncture between exposition and middle section; and in the coda.

Mm. 24/4–92. The remainder of the exposition elaborates the C and D motifs but also brings reminiscences of the Adagio motif B (from m. 8) at mm. 37–40. The large-scale second group begins at m. 55, in G-flat major (G-flat = F-sharp, the pitch to which the C figure of the Adagio moves in m. 7 on its way to G), and the importance of G-flat major as primary contrasting tonality is confirmed by the change of key signature at m. 71, which holds to the end of the exposition.

Middle section (development)

Mm. 93/3–103. This passage links the exposition and development sections; it elaborates and condenses the contrasts of the original Adagio and Allegro (mm. 1–19). The A1 segment returns in an abbreviated form (mm. 93/3–95) in G-flat major, followed by a one-measure outburst (m. 96) that combines the Allegro C and D motifs and that re-spells G-flat major as F-sharp major.

The short Allegro in turn gives way to another return of A2 (mm. 97/3–99) in D major, a key that is then confirmed at once by the same fragment combining the Allegro C and D motifs (m. 100). The colors and textures are kaleidoscopic: low registers for the Adagio; middle-high ones for the Allegro. And now the two-note rising figure in the cello at m. 99 emerges again in a brief Adagio moment at mm. 101–103, paving the way for the rest of the development section. This figure remains as an ostinato rhythm all the way through this section, joined at first with the D motif in violin 1 (mm. 105–106), then with a lyrical new theme in the cello (mm. 106–107). Both elements remain in play throughout the middle section, with only a wisp of the Allegro C motif heard three times (at mm. 105, 109, and 115), hardly more than memory traces. The basic harmonic pattern of the middle section is simple enough, moving down through four steps of the circle of fifths (D major—G major—C minor—V/B-flat) and thus arriving at the home dominant to prepare for the return to B-flat major and the recapitulation at m. 132.

Recapitulation

Mm. 132–213. As in some other later works, the recapitulation of the Allegro (significantly, without any Adagio material) is not gradually prepared, but grows suddenly and swiftly out of the sixth and last appearance of the lyrical theme of the middle section, restating the C and D combination of the Allegro in fortissimo and elaborating the running groups of four sixteenth-notes (the C theme). These figures appear in contrary motion in the lower strings while the violin 1 brings the D figure in high register, an octave higher than its original statement at m. 15 and a fourth higher than at m. 25. From here on the "recapitulation" is really a free adaptation of exposition material, not a repetition of it. Marvelous moments abound, among them the unprecedented augmented-triad harmony at m. 140, in sudden piano dynamic. The second group, formerly in G-flat major, now reappears in D-flat major; Beethoven makes room for a greatly expanded twofold restatement, first in D-flat major, as a parallel to the G-flat major of the exposition (mm. 160–172), then in the tonic, B-flat major (172–183). The extended restatement of the second group, with its intimate lyricism in *sotto voce,* lifts the movement to a new expressivity. The elaborations of the Allegro figures that had been heard earlier in G-flat major (mm. 71/4–92) are now firmly in B-flat major but are rescored and newly configured, remaining just recognizable enough to remind us that we are hearing a recapitulation, while really forming an imaginative reconstruction of the original material. At mm. 206–209 the violin 1 soars into the stratosphere, reaching a high D at 209, from which it drops precipitously to the two-octave range of the original A2 figure (B-flat unison in all strings) to end the recapitulation.

Coda

The coda (mm. 213/4–234) is the summation toward which the movement has been pointing since the Adagio-Allegro contrasts of its opening. At m. 213 the original one-octave B-flat unison sonority of the opening reappears, and even though its role is to close the Allegro recapitulation, its pitch-sequence is the same as the first two notes of the opening of the movement (B-flat—A), whereupon the Adagio opening phrase re-emerges in full form, with both A1 and A2 phrases (213/4–217/2). These phrases are now both raised up an octave, allowing for an immediate link to the Allegro C theme, which starts its rapid descent from that same B-flat (m. 218), then returns to the Adagio after only one measure and moves up from B-natural to C (m. 219). The upward surge continues with another Allegro-Adagio alternation, and at m. 221 the Adagio picks up the high C and moves up chromatically to D. Insistently, the same Allegro figures return again, beginning from the D that has now been reached, and moving forward and upward in a beautiful cadential passage up to G (m. 224), from where a final statement of the Allegro C and D motives, smoothly combined in pianissimo, can bring the movement to a close, *sempre pp* except for the final cadence in forte.

This coda fully realizes the potential of the upward two-note figure that has been haunting the movement since m. 4 (the cadential close of A2) and which has persisted through myriad transformations. In the coda the chromatic scalar rise of the two-note figure, as the Adagio and Allegro tempi alternate every measure, is the culmination of the upward motion from B-flat to F that had been heard in mm. 1–7, now dramatized as never before.

At what stage of composition did Beethoven see that the movement's opening figures could give rise to a coda that would so fully realize their potential? In the Moscow sketchbook we find a sketch for this coda that gives us the answer (ex. 4). Here Beethoven writes "Ende" over the sketch, showing that he is thinking about how to end the movement. He begins with the A1 figure (significantly in the A2 register, as in the final version of the coda), and follows it with A2 in the higher octave (again as in the final version). Next comes the descending Allegro theme C, followed immediately by the rising B-flat–B-natural–C and then an abbreviated notation for the next Allegro descent. This is enough to make clear that the form of the coda

Ex. 4. Sketch for the coda, showing the Adagio phrases A1 and A2 in their proper registers, interruptions of the Allegro material, and rising chromatic motion in the violin 1 part, and ending with the words "Steigt sempre" (Moscow sketchbook, p. 44, st. 4–5).

was conceived very early. Clinching this interpretation are the two words "Steigt sempre" ("always rising"), showing that the remaining rising pattern, from C through D and up to G (final version, mm. 223–224), was already in his mind before the many remaining elements and details of the movement had been worked out. The sketch fulfills our intuitive assumption that Beethoven must have imagined the basic outline of this movement first. It reminds us of what Beethoven meant when he wrote, in another context, "it is my custom, even in instrumental music, to keep the whole in view."

It comes as no surprise that some of Beethoven's earlier codas have the same role as this one: to fulfill thematic and motivic implications that have been left unresolved until the end of the movement, to serve the role that has been called "thematic completion."[9] This movement is a supreme example of such "completion" in Beethoven's works, and it enables us to understand how the transcendental "late style" is rooted in his earlier achievements.

CONVERSATION

JS: Joel Smirnoff (violin 1); **RC**: Ronald Copes (violin 2); **SR**: Samuel Rhodes (viola); **JK**: Joel Krosnick (cello); **LL**: Lewis Lockwood

SR In a very different way from opus 18 no. 1, the essence of this movement is in the first two bars and that half-cadence, or in the first four bars and then the resolution to the cadence at bar 4 with the subito pianos in between. That idea, which is expanded all the way through the piece, especially at crucial places—the beginning of the development section and the coda—that's the idea of the introduction. Then there's the idea of integrating the slow introduction with the fast music of the allegro and the themes associated with it, and the interplay and unification of the material between both. The challenge for the performer is how to juggle between the two tempi coherently, and all the different ways to express what we hope is something close to what Beethoven wanted.

JK And this isn't the first time he's done this, right? Opus 127, he sort of did it.

LL But not the same way, because there you have the slow introduction coming three times but not in quite the same way.

JK Yes, but not integrated back and forth.

LL It has its own dramatic and inherent complexities.

SR Here he makes the introductory material a much more integral part of the piece all the way through. The standard way an introduction would be used in a symphony, and more rarely in a string quartet, is to have a small passage of music start off, either with uncertainty or with something quiet, and then go to a fast full sonata movement. The introduction would stand by itself without reference to the main section of the movement.

RC *A la* the "Dissonant" quartet [Mozart K. 465].

SR Exactly. Whereas here, the attempt is to make the introduction an integral part of the piece thematically, and at times to fuse it with the fast music later on in the development and the recapitulation.

JK I find this huge long line in this introduction between the opening and bar 7 with the subito pianos extraordinary, especially that long slur for the cello through the first of them [mm. 2–3]—saying "Hey, it can't stop." That it's not a contradiction in his mind to write a subito piano and a slur sustaining through it. And then the second subito piano [m. 4] is then the start of the second half of the phrase. So it's really an extraordinary use of these subito pianos that we spoke of earlier.

LL Yes, and the piano again at the end of the next phrase, the crescendo to the forte in 6 and the diminuendo to piano on the downbeat of 7.

SR Taking just that cadential fragment and using it as the basis of the development section, later on, is quite an extraordinary idea. And of course taking it up in the coda again [m. 214], and this time, with the interruption of the material, through that allowing the line to continue to climb up as far as it will go, and rounding off the piece from that moment.

LL In a movement as densely packed with complications as this, when you coach young performers what do you find to be some of their problems of getting access to what's in here?

JS Well, one of the problems with this piece, as a performer, is the key. B-flat is a hard key for a quartet to tune up for various reasons; one is to get the open strings to work throughout as thirds and sevenths. Of course, the piece goes to very remote keys like G-flat major for its second subject, instead of going to the V. But if you look for instance at the second allegro [mm. 24ff], you've got a long, long bunch of music ending in bar 36 which is all sixteenth-notes except for one voice, and all the harmonic information is in those sixteenth-notes. So it's very hard to make it harmonically clear where the cadences are, where the tensions are—it demands a great deal both from the listener and the quartet to try to provide clarity. Even after that, as it moves to piano and figures are being thrown around, there's a clear harmonic scheme to it, before one finally gets the clarity of the unison at 45, but it's obscured by the busy quality of it, and that's what's hard.

JK Very hard. It's easy to get something terribly slow and stagnant and then terribly fast and nervous, but as Joel is saying there are things inside this allegro. I don't know how serious he was about it, but Mr. Lehner [Eugene Lehner, violist in the Kolisch Quartet and mentor to the original Juilliard Quartet] used to suggest that this allegro was definitely not as fast as we played it. He wanted to hear the adagio. He didn't want the allegro at the same tempo, but he wanted it slower.

SR The answer, sort of—

JK Some thought that it's not necessarily black and white. You know, as Joel is saying, there is a tremendous amount of harmonic information carried in the allegro, which means you can't use, for example, a normal textbook spiccato. There's a very interesting sense of non legato and not staccato.

JS He's looking for clarity in ensemble when he says "non ligato." But for me this rough-and-tumble quality gives it an orchestral quality—it's close to his orchestral textures, which are murky in this particular way. For me this first movement has an overture-like quality to it, more than almost any other piece, because the themes are not even that memorable once the piece gets going. And it's going to be a very long journey to the end of the Grosse Fuge, God knows, with three different scherzos and a cavatina: one gets lost in this piece. Somehow for me, this movement is a prelude, more than almost any other movement in Beethoven—also because of the way that it ends, which is not with a great sense of resolution but with a sense of expectation. It's a rather abrupt ending, for that matter, and a jovial, witty ending, which is unexpected.

JK   There's something else that plays into that. This half-step side-slip up from the dominant [mm. 51–52] is as though you can refer, as in an overture, to something that's going to be in the second scene, because this key of G-flat is going to be dealt with in the second scherzo, all these flat keys.

SR   Also in the second part of the Grosse Fuge.

JK   So in a way there's an overture indicating what's to come later, and that's a spectacular moment in this piece. That's what, in a way, what all those sforzandi are about and the fortes in bars 45 to 48: to say, here's the dominant, here's the dominant, here's the dominant—which I'm about to destroy. And then an extraordinary moment in 51 and 52.

LL   Moving up chromatically.

JS   But in reality there's not that much material in this piece.

LL   No, it's short, compact, and dense.

JS   He puts out a couple of ideas and he makes this texture, this kind of tapestry out of them. And then he gives your first allegro in legato in a kind of dolce, which is very wonderful, and also has a patient quality about it. I'm talking about 71. I always think of for some reason—I've said this to Sam and to the quartet—there's a sense of *Meistersinger,* of a Wagnerian sense of patience about some of this. And that particular section starting at 71, it sits in this wonderful place. Not an Italian place, by the way; we haven't addressed the move from Italy back to a more German language, from the opus 18s, which exist more in an Italian style, to something which becomes much more rooted in its own environment.

LL   By the way, the sudden change of key signature to G-flat in 71 could at least be questioned, since the piece has been in G-flat for quite a while.

JS   We've talked about that.

JK   You mean why the key change is not in 55.

JS   This is something I talk about when I coach, too. We're very interested in the moment of modulation, but at what point does the listener or the player become convinced of the legitimacy of the new key? Because he moves very suspiciously, chromatically, to G-flat, as Joel Krosnick has said, by going to its dominant at bar 53, and then it's not terribly well advocated—we're waiting for the shoe to drop to move away from it. The sequence starting in bar 66 is dubious too. Finally, when he gives you that key signature at 71, he's saying: "Okay, I'm committing myself to G-flat major and this is where we're going to stay."

JK The cello has V–I at that moment, not a chromatic side-slip as before.

JS It's one thing to modulate to a key; it's another thing to really believe you're going to stay there and be committed to it. I think that's the moment.

SR If that's so, then why is there a key signature change to A-flat at 160 and to B-flat at 173?

JS Because we've heard it already.

LL I think he's not in the key of A-flat, it's in D-flat.

JS That's true. [*laughs*]

SR In D-flat, and yet he changes the key signature to A-flat. Why does he do that?

LL There are some late Beethoven places, and even late-middle, where he's one accidental short of what he should be. The Eighth Symphony finale is such a case. There's a passage in F-sharp minor but it's only got two sharps. This happens in Baroque music sometimes, that you're one flat short.

SR Usually in a minor key, like C minor with two flats.

JK There's a quality about this being sure. You see this in Bach dance movements where you're moving from tonic to dominant: I'll do it—but let me just be sure that you understood me—I'll do it again; and maybe on the third time it's irrevocable.

LL Is Bach doubting that people will understand what he's doing?

JK I don't know. It's dramatic, the moves from tonic to the dominant, and then dominant to a resolution, to the relative minor, to . . . These things are underlined in the way Joel was saying, especially the first move.

JS It's also possible the way he wrote the recap, when he put in those keys, he realized: "Gee, I don't really have to sit around writing accidentals all day long. I can make life easier for myself." He learned. [*laughter*]

SR So why didn't he put in the fifth accidental?

JS You know, the cello lands on a G-flat [m. 160]. But it's a diminished chord, which is really an A-flat-7. The second violin has a suspension which moves to a B-double-flat, which eventually resolves in the viola.

LL That's it. It's a good enharmonic moment to write B-double-flat rather than A.

I have something else to offer you for this movement, which I found to my own astonishment in the Moscow sketchbook, a pencil sketchbook for this whole movement and also opus 132. The coda has fascinated me for years because you have the reorganization of the opening material into the higher octave, the adagio stuff at 214, and then comes the allegro running down, and now you stop and you begin running up chromatically in adagio, and you start the allegro again, and you do it again chromatically, and then you come to this final moment, which to me is very beautiful and rather poignant.

JS   Absolutely.

LL   The sketch is marked "Ende," meaning the end of the movement, and it consists of nothing but a telegraphic version of what you see in the first violin part: the adagio stuff in the right octaves and then the little allegro stuff, and the adagio again, and the allegro again, and the adagio. All as it is, but in telegraphic form, and at the bottom he writes the words "steigt sempre," always rising, which is a verbal statement of the feeling that he wants you to have, that he has in his head, about how this works. Going up by steps—which is the motif from the beginning which, as you say, Sam, generates the development. So I thought it was wonderful to find a synoptic sketch that gives the whole coda, just what I wanted it to do, explains everything, and it's the real stuff.

JS   One of my favorite moments is this little plagal cadence that happens from 226 into 227, major into minor.

LL Yes, that's gorgeous.

JS There's something very poignant about that. You go to the top of the line in the middle of 224, but then coming down and going plagal for a moment into the last little cadence—I love that. And subito piano, of course, which draws attention to it, as Ron says; it draws your attention to a particularly poignant moment.

SR And we have a wavy line in the half-bar before that, the second beat.

JS Yeah, we make sure that you hear it. We clobber you with it. [*laughter*]

LL I was very interested in what you said before about feeling the movement as something like an overture, in the Baroque sense, because "Overture" is, of course, the term that he uses for the Grosse Fuge. In the starting allegro here, you have a rapid sixteenth-note theme and a distinctive theme in quarter-notes and eighth-notes against it [m. 15], which is a very rare combination. In a way it telegraphs what will happen in the Grosse Fuge.

JS Wonderful. Actually, if you look specifically at the coda, it is very much presaging the Grosse Fuge, because the Grosse Fuge is syncopated, and here you have this emphasis on 2s and 4s, as you will have them in the Grosse Fuge—in 218, 220, and 222.

SR On another topic: there is always a difficulty in this movement of bridging the two tempos, the adagio ma non troppo and the allegro. One of the interesting places that we chose to illustrate that is from 209 into the statement of the adagio at 214. The way it turns out, at least for us, the adagio is just a little bit more than twice as slow as the allegro; and there is a calando through that phrase from 209, especially as it gets into the longer notes in the augmentation. So the last quarter-note of 213 is equal to an eighth-note of the adagio. And in that way we avoid setting the adagio. We make it more of a piece with the rest of the movement, so it makes a transition.

JS So the last quarter-note becomes the eighth-note upbeat. That's how we do it.

SR Yeah, that's indicated.

JK Since that arises from pianissimo, we go into the piano in the second bar.

SR We don't make a subito piano; for once we go straight ahead through. But then, of course, in the next phrase we don't; we go above piano and stop. And then make the repeated lower-octave upbeat—it's an upbeat to the allegro actually—each time a little bit more suspended and taking more time. And then the allegro snaps you out of it, and then you're suspended even more, and then the allegro snaps you out of it again, and you go to the end.

JK These moments of difficulty of going back and forth between the allegro and the adagio are there right at the beginning, at bar 20, for example. The adagio starts on the downbeat. It's not set in advance. Same thing at the moment of 97: the end of the allegro is the beginning of the adagio.

JS One thing I find unique about this movement is the way the music kind of breaks down at the front of the development. In this quick alternation of tempo, adagio and allegro, there is a lot of thinking going on here, rather than action.

LL Yes, re-contemplation.

JS It's an important moment, until finally the piece decides where it wants to go. And where it wants to go is, of course, very interesting.

SR Also he comes up with this theme in the cello that's like the second theme yet it's something new [m. 106].

RC Right, it is new material.

JK It's something new.

SR It's warming and inspiring, like the sun coming out.

JK I'm thinking second theme, but aside from what forces it to be new, what the hell is a second theme doing in this context? It feels like the strangest thing.

LL Yes, it's very strange. The second theme after all came out of the first two measures.

JK Yeah, but at the same time: [*sings cello part, mm. 106–107*]

LL I see: it's another step up but it feels so new because it's as if it's almost in a different piece.

RC An awful lot of it has to do with the context, because two measures before it just feels weird—completely new material.

JK I feel so strange in this place.

LL You still do? Still strange after all these years? [*laughter*]

JK You're supposed to.

JS But what I love about this transition into the allegro: in the last three bars there is obviously this thought process that says, "Okay, I'm going to focus on this resolution"—

SR "How should I say this?"

JS —"and that's what I'm going to decide." It's almost as if you watch the creative process at work.

RC But there's a strong sense of improvisation here.

LL This degree of newness in a piece as condensed and molecular as this movement is very striking to me and remains striking. And therefore it demands a higher level of explanation—which nobody's got yet. [*laughter*]

JK Well, everything that we are talking about here is unsolvable. You just have to listen. I heard a performance of opus 130 and the fugue by the Mendelssohn Quartet, with Bobby [Robert Mann] playing first violin for them because they were in between first violinists. And it's not only that intellectually this is the summa, or emotionally. I was listening to this piece and I thought: "My God, I have never heard anything so complex in my life." We're inside when we play it, but I was sitting there listening and thinking, "How can anybody understand it?" and I looked at the audience, and people were transfixed. Everyone was getting their own understanding. And these were not musicians. I was experiencing how complicated it was and how complex, and as I was looking around I thought: "The audience is telling you that somehow this transcends knowing what's happening"—the difficulties of structure, the motivic thing . . .

RC They didn't move very much during it.

JK I watched and nobody was breathing.

JS I was thinking about the late quartets generally; for me, each one of them has a slow movement which is really, in a sense, the key. This goes way back to before Beethoven even, but slow movements often function as problem-solving movements in some way. You slow things down so that you can examine them and solve them. And also all the lates have a very abrupt ending, even the Grosse Fuge in its funny way: "I've said what I need to say. I'm not going to give you a big blasting ending with a lot of cadences. I've said it, that's it."

JK You know: [*sings last 3 bars of op. 131*]

JS It's true of every single one of them, in its own way; the levitation in 6/8 of opus 127 is a light ending. It's not an attempt to be heroic. It's an attempt to say—"Good-bye." [*laughter*]

SR As opposed to the opus 59s.

JS Which build and build, and then wham-o!

LL Yes, the building up to a heroic finale is a middle-period thing.

JK We work again and again and again and again and again on the ending of 131.

JS Well, that's a particularly interesting one, of course.

JK To build down into the ending of that: [*sings last 4 bars*]

JS It's never played in the original rhythm, of course. The actual rhythm [of the final three chords] is twice as fast.

JK And the audience always . . . [*claps tentatively*]

LL They're not sure that it's the ending.

JK *We're* never sure.

JS But it's true of all of them: opus 132 is another ending that's very difficult for the audience to quite get.

SR The one that maybe it's most true of is opus 95.

LL Well, that is a problem of problems.

SR Right, a conundrum.

JK Well, 74 ain't so clear either.

LL No, but at least it doesn't have the enormous contrast of affect that you find in opus 95.

JS I don't have a problem with it.

LL No, but there are people who do.

JS Because if you look at *Egmont,* it explains it.

LL But in *Egmont* it's heroic, it's victory.

JK There were composers I knew when I was first playing 95 who said about the ending: "How could he do this? He ruined the piece!"

LL People talk this way, they do.

JK "He wrecked the piece!"

SR It's the Berlioz reaction to the end of Donna Anna's aria in *Don Giovanni.* He was appalled by that ending, the fast part. The last movement of the G minor quintet [K. 516] would be a similar kind of thing.

LL Lightness of being was in the world long before Kundera thought of it—and we wouldn't have 135 if it weren't for that.

JS You're bringing up a subject much bigger than the end of opus 135, which is that composers in their worst adversity, on their deathbeds, can write very jolly pieces.

LL No question about it.

JS I think of Bartók writing the third piano concerto for his wife, and writing a fugue at the end that goes [*sings*] while he's dying. What a great act of generosity that is. That's the real heroic, to be allegro in the face of dying.

LL That is the question: "Muss es sein?" The question is asked in *grave,* but the answer is given in allegro.

JS Exactly. That's very Mozartian, of course: ask a serious question and give a silly answer. That goes back a few years.

SR It's not silly, though.

JS Not silly, but with levity.

LL There is a quotation I saw about the late quartets which I kept for years, from 1993. That's the year in which a Princeton mathematician, Andrew Wiles, solved Fermat's last theorem. It had been around for 350 years and nobody had ever been able to solve it, and he provides a solution. One of his colleagues from the Princeton mathematics department, Simon Kochen, was quoted as saying, "This is an achievement about which I can say: we are living in its time"—meaning this is an achievement of such magnitude in mathematics that we are lucky to be around when it happens. Then he says, "It's like listening to the late Beethoven string quartets." [*laughter*] So I thought, this will do for a while.

JS I have to say, in terms of the emotional world of the late quartets, there's no question that there's a lot of looking backward from Beethoven's point of view, as in the fugue in opus 131. And also prayer. It functions both in that piece and in the "Heiliger Dankgesang" [op. 132, 3rd mvt.].

SR Especially in the background parts.

JS It's quite explicit: the idea of using the modal quality for that movement, and ending it as it does. It's a definite looking upward. One has to partake of that entirely, and experience it by the way, in order for it to work. And what a great thing that is.

JK In the Heiligenstadt Testament, he said that he felt himself to be in contact with God—and then the conundrum of "but He's made me deaf."

JS Because of the deafness, because of the abstract quality of the music, there's something ideal expressed—in the Platonic sense, as in the *Republic*. I think that's why your mathematician said what he did. There is an ideal expression and a picture of life as we would like it to be lived and felt, as we wish that it could be.

LL And these pieces were absolutely not understood when they were new. The opus 59 had some trouble getting accepted, but not much; no. 2 took a while. By the 1820s opus 59 was part of the basic literature, but these pieces needed another thirty years. And even in the early twentieth century, I remember

Roger Sessions saying that in his early days these were still regarded as difficult to understand by musicians.

SR The Grosse Fuge was not played as part of the Beethoven cycle by many groups up to fairly recently. The Joachim Quartet as far as I know—I've seen programs of their concerts—never played it. And the Budapest [Quartet] maybe played it as a separate piece but never as part of opus 130.

LL No, that wasn't the way, except for Kolisch and his tradition.

SR And of course we did.

JK I still remember the first professional quartet that I played it with, the Iowa Quartet, playing a performance in Iowa City. The University of Iowa had Imre Waldbauer on the faculty in the late 1930s, from the Waldbauer-Kerpoly Quartet, which commissioned the second Bartók quartet, so that community had a strong chamber music background. I remember taking part in what I guess was the first performance of the Grosse Fuge there, in the early 1960s, and a lot of people came backstage saying, "I don't get it. What is this?"

LL You probably know that recently James Levine did it with the BSO string section, twice.

SR Is that so?

LL At the beginning of the program, with the two violin concertos, Beethoven and Schoenberg, in the middle, and then ending with it again. And I hear that a certain number of people were saying, "Uh, we heard this already, why are you doing it again?" [*laughter*] Once was enough.

Earlier in this session you were talking about the depth of these pieces. When you have a group of 18-year-olds who want to work on a piece like this, how do you get them—

JK Into the realm of the materials?

RC Well, you can. You can certainly talk about it. In some respects something like the "Heiliger Dankgesang" is the easiest, because the spiritual elements are so present, so clear at the surface. But in all of them it has a lot to do with trying to understand his point of view, his circumstances. I don't know how deeply young people, or any of us for that matter, can relate to those circumstances, but we all have at least an abstract appreciation of the fact that it was an awful lot to be dealing with, so there is some kind of empathetic potential there, at least.

SR The point is just to get them to think about the different elements. For example, last week I heard a group—this wasn't a student group; this was a formed quartet that has had quite a bit of professional experience, especially with contemporary music—but they were playing opus 132 for the first time, and they played the march and the last movement. And I asked them afterward about the march, because there was something I thought they missed about the way they played it. A close friend of ours, who is not a professional musician, but somebody who loves music deeply and goes to many, many concerts, came up with the question: After something like the "Heiliger Dankgesang," how could he write a march like that? What did he have in mind? Why did he write that? I can't understand such banal music suddenly coming in there. And I asked him to think about that and try to answer that question, and maybe that would provide some insight.

JK All the elements we've talked about in opus 130—the one thing you certainly can do with students is to get them into the room with each of these elements. You work on them individually and get the five or six things that are in this work, including the key areas and various things. If you really get them in the room with those materials and then back them up and say: "Okay, now go from one to the other but don't just go. Really be there and see what happens to you." If you can get them to experience the magnitude of the difficulty of going from one to the other, then I'm not against somebody saying to an audience from a point of view of youth: "My God, look at this material, look at how hard it is." And they may say something that's remarkable.

RC That's my point concerning young people playing these late quartets: I don't know that the performance will reflect quite the same values that older, more mature musicians might reflect. But for a quartet of young musicians today to be exposed and to deal with these difficulties intimately, really to deal with them, what does that give them thirty years from now?

The fact is, we all did play these quartets when we were young. We all learned them when we were young, and that helps us understand them in a way that just age or experience doesn't.

JS Usually when a student group comes to you and says, "We want to play opus 131," it's because they heard it somewhere and they fell in love with it. And I think the best incentive to learning is love. If you are so taken with something that you just—with me, I just put the needle down over and over until the record didn't sound like anything anymore. But I fell in love with opus 131 at a very, very young age, and knew that one certainly the best of any of the lates, so when I came to the chair and they said, "Which late do you want to do this year?" I said "131." And so it's possible to know these pieces and love these pieces as a young person without necessarily having even played them. In the best of circumstances the students will come to you with that attitude, understanding that the remote mountaintop in the clouds resides somewhere that they don't quite know, but they see part of that mountain.

JK And if they go with great love in their hearts in seeking some voice for their love, they may then give the audience something. Just the effort of going, if they go.

You know, what used to bother me very much, coaching chamber music at Juilliard: when a group came in, one of those top groups at Juilliard—concertmasters and things like that—they could practically read the Debussy quartet. And they could read probably anything, in a certain way better than we can play it. I remember this is early in my history with the Juilliard Quartet, second year; I wasn't so confident about coaching pieces, and I thought, "What should I say?" They read it well, they were sure of themselves, but they really couldn't understand what it means. But how do you say it? They played all the notes, they played the rhythms, they played pretty well in tune. How do you slow them down and say: "Hey! Listen to the words you're saying—you're not hearing anything you're saying."

RC That concept of musical language: I think students typically think of the comparison of music to language as being very esoteric—music just has meanings that are universal—instead of understanding that there are so many linguistic components: there are elements of syntax, there are vocabulary elements, with rhythm and harmony and so forth. All of these create a kind of meaning that's very specific, that's not general. It's important to figure out how to use that meaning to inspire so many elements of what it is that you say: crescendos, articulations, dynamics . . .

LL We live in a culture in which expectations about experience, from films and so much else, are that there is a change every ten seconds—novelty and immediate gratification of all kinds— so it's very hard to get people to sit down with you for a long-range experience.

JS It's a problem from our point of view—to find an audience that really will go with you for the length of time. For one movement, we're talking about maybe fifteen minutes or so. But to be able to sit there—

JK Especially when we take the repeat in 130.

JS Well, actually I have a problem with that repeat myself. [*laughs*]

JK The problem is, how long will an audience stay there? It makes tremendous demands on them.

JS I have a hard time with that repeat. I find it very difficult to bring off because of the alterations of the movement.

JK I feel it very difficult to bring off that repeat also. I feel that I shouldn't even try. [*laughs*] But it sure changes the piece an enormous amount if you don't take the repeat.

SR I agree.

LL It needs the length.

RC It does.

JK Just an attempt by the audience to hear the material, which is full of enormously enigmatic conflicts the whole time. I even feel it as a formula: Let's try this again.

LL But the coda, by reflection, should make it clear.

JK Except it doesn't end pianissimo—it ends [*sings last three notes*].

LL   Well, it's not the end of the work, it's the end of that movement.

JK   That's the overture aspect of it. And also the whole structure of this piece: an overture, three scherzi, a prayer—and God help us. [*laughter*]

LL   Beethoven the great democrat, the great believer that all men are created brothers, was waiting once while the first performance of 130 with the fugue took place. Afterward he asked, "How did it go?" and they were trying to explain that the Cavatina and the Alla danza tedesca went great, and he says "And the fugue?" They had to say something, so they said, "Not as much." "Cattle! Asses!" [*laughter*] That's the report, anyway. Chances are it's right.

SR   But he agreed to change it, nonetheless?

LL   Yes, but that's another long, complicated story. It's always finales that get changed, by the way—the Kreutzer Sonata, and he even agreed with the Hammerklavier Sonata that in England they could just publish two movements if they wanted to, and publish the other two movements as a separate piece. So all sorts of, to us, bizarre possibilities seem to have gone through his head.

JK   It always seemed to me commercial; the publishers put it to him: "You know, it's a very long last movement and you could publish it separately and make more money."

LL They did. He was in terrible straits at this time.

JS In general, I would say that when you play the late quartets—which of course is the high point of one's musical career, if one gets to perform this with a wonderful group of musicians—I can only speak for myself—[*laughter*]

JK Hear, hear.

JS But it's a great, great experience, and of course, it's a deepening experience personally: it demands that one go into the world of a very deep mind and a deeply feeling person. One has to be worthy of these pieces, in a sense. And there is also the issue: can one play these at a very young age? Probably not. The sense of being able to look back over a life, of being able to consider life from a patient viewpoint, of being able to look mortality in the face—this is all part of the expression of these pieces. Also the ability to think abstractly: because the man, removed from his world by deafness and writing for his most abstract medium, which is the quartet, contributes to an expression which levitates in terms of abstraction. So it places demands upon the player which go way beyond the technical, and maybe to the emotional and the spiritual, certainly.

SR And also the physical, by the way: the physical workout of playing an all-Beethoven concert, a whole program of a Beethoven cycle, let's say. There's nothing that tires me out more, in both the spiritual and the physical sense. My arm feels like I can't play another note.

JK   I still remember a moment in my first year in the quartet. I had played opus 135 before, but what I had never done is play it at the end of a cycle. We were rehearsing somewhere in San Francisco, flying through the cycle for the first time with me. And we had played everything, it was the final program, but we hadn't played 135 in a while. And I hadn't played it in the context of the cycle and I just fell apart. [*Sings theme in mm. 4–5 of first movement of op. 135*] This is what it all is in the end—it's this? I felt as though I had never heard 135 before.

LL   Many people—laymen, musicians, everybody—agree that these works represent a summa of what the art form was capable of. From your point of view, from the inside performing them, do you continue to have that feeling about them?

SR   There's no question about it.

ANNOTATED SCORE

Opus 130, first movement

From *Inside Beethoven's Quartets: History, Performance, Interpretation*, by Lewis Lockwood and the Juilliard String Quartet (Harvard University Press, 2008), copyright © 2008 by the President and Fellows of Harvard College.

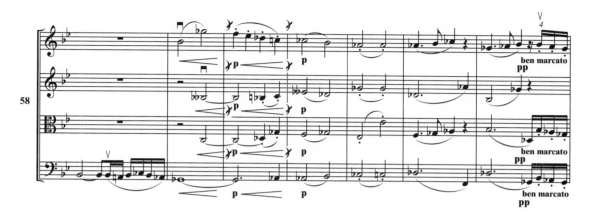

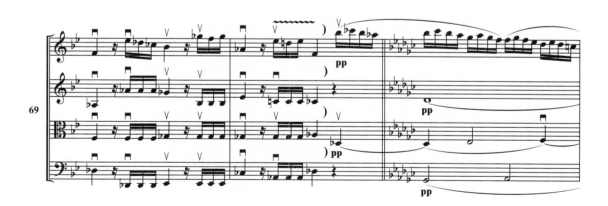

APPENDIX

NOTES

ACKNOWLEDGMENTS

INDEX

APPENDIX

Opus 18 no. 1, first movement (Amenda version)

OPUS 18 NO. 1 (AMENDA VERSION)

OPUS 18 NO. 1 (AMENDA VERSION)

NOTES

ABBREVIATIONS

AMZ	*Allgemeine Musikalische Zeitung* (Leipzig, 1798–1848)
Anderson	*The Letters of Beethoven,* ed. Emily Anderson, 3 vols. (London, 1961)
BF	*Beethoven Forum* (University of Nebraska Press, 1992–2001; University of Illinois Press, 1999–2007)
BML	Lewis Lockwood, *Beethoven: The Music and the Life* (New York, 2003)
Briefwechsel	Beethoven, *Briefwechsel Gesamtausgabe,* ed. Sieghard Brandenburg, 7 vols. (Munich, 1996–1998)
JTW	Douglas Johnson, Alan Tyson, and Robert Winter, *The Beethoven Sketchbooks: History, Reconstruction, Inventory* (Berkeley, 1985)
Kinsky-Halm	*Das Werk Beethovens: Thematisch-Bibliographisches Verzeichnis seiner Saemtlichen Vollendeten Kompositionen,* ed. Georg Kinsky and Hans Halm (Munich, 1955)
N II	G. Nottebohm, *Zweite Beethoveniana* (Leipzig, 1887; rept. New York, 1970)

TF	Alexander Wheelock Thayer, *Thayer's Life of Beethoven,* rev. and ed. Elliot Forbes (Princeton, 1964)
Wegeler-Ries	Franz Gerhard Wegeler and Ferdinand Ries, *Biographische Notizen über Ludwig van Beethoven* (Coblenz, 1838; rept. New York, 1972)

THE OPUS 18 QUARTETS

1. Ignaz von Seyfried, *Ludwig van Beethovens Studien im Generalbass . . . ,* 2nd rev. ed., edited by H. H. Pierson (Leipzig, 1853), appendix, "Ludwig van Beethoven: Eine Biographische Skizze," pp. 6ff. This translation of the first part of the passage slightly modifies that in *BML*, pp. 312–313. Originally published in 1832, these remarks were apparently written between 1830 and 1832, as we learn from the autograph manuscript of Seyfried's biographical sketch, which was described in a sale catalogue by Lüder H. Niemayer, Bonn, in 1990. The death dates of Schuppanzigh (2 March 1830) and Franz Weiss (25 January 1830), plus the publication date of 1832, show that Seyfried wrote this portion of the sketch after March 1830 and before 1832. For more on Seyfried, see Bettina von Seyfried, *Ignaz Ritter von Seyfried, Thematisch-Bibliographisches Verzeichnis, Aspekte der Biographie und des Werkes* (Frankfurt, 1990).

2. The main example is op. 18 no. 5 in relation to Mozart's K. 464 in the same key. See James Webster, "Traditional Elements in Beethoven's Middle-Period String Quartets," in R. Winter and B. Carr, eds., *Beethoven: Performers and Critics* (Detroit, 1980), pp. 94–133; on the "Harp" quartet op. 74, see Nicholas Marston, "'Haydn's Geist aus Beethovens Händen?'—Fantasy and Farewell in the Quartet in E-flat, Op. 74," in W. Kinderman, ed., *The String Quartets of Beethoven* (Urbana, Ill., 2006), pp. 109–131.

3. TF, p. 305. In the Testament, addressed to his brothers Carl and (though he is not named) Johann, Beethoven wrote, "I would like the instruments from Prince L[ichnowsky] to be preserved by one of you, but not to be

the cause of strife between you, and as soon as they can serve you a better purpose, sell them." The fate of the four instruments from Lichnowsky is uncertain. For a long time the four instruments now preserved in the Musikinstrumenten-Museum of the Staatliches Institut für Musikforschung, Berlin, on permanent loan from Bonn, were thought to be the ones given by Lichnowsky, but recent research suggests that they are not. It appears that Beethoven owned other stringed instruments in the course of his life. See Kai Köpp, "Beethovens Violoncello—Ein Geschenk des Fürsten Lichnowsky?—Zur Provenienz der Streichquartett-Instrumente Beethovens," in *Beethovens Werke für Klavier und Violoncello,* ed. Sieghard Brandenburg, Ingeborg Maass, and Wolfgang Osthoff (Bonn, 2004), pp. 305–353.

4. See *BML,* pp. 80ff; and Anton Schindler, *Beethoven As I Knew Him,* ed. and trans. Donald W. MacArdle (Chapel Hill, 1966), pp. 59 and 84 n. 35.

5. Schindler, *Beethoven As I Knew Him,* p. 57f.

6. See Ludwig Finscher, *Studien zur Geschichte des Streichquartetts,* vol. 1 (Kassel, 1974), and its review by James Webster in *Journal of the American Musicological Society* 28 (1975): 543–549; see also James Webster, *Haydn's "Farewell" Symphony and the Idea of Classical Style* (Cambridge, England, 1991). A useful survey is Paul Griffiths, *The String Quartet: A History* (New York, 1983).

7. For example, the first movement of the quartet op. 59 no. 3; the *Leonore* overtures nos. 2 and 3; and the quartet op. 74.

8. See Douglas Johnson, "1794–1795: Decisive Years in Beethoven's Early Development," *Beethoven Studies 3,* ed. Alan Tyson (Cambridge, England, 1982), pp. 1–28, esp. pp. 2–13 on Beethoven's transformation of the early wind octet (later published as op. 103) into his string quintet op. 4.

9. See Sieghard Brandenburg, "Beethoven's op. 12 Violin Sonatas: On the Path to His Personal Style," in Lewis Lockwood and Mark Kroll, eds., *The Beethoven Violin Sonatas: History, Criticism, Performance* (Urbana, Ill., 2004), pp. 5–23.

10. For the dedication, written in French to Count Johann Georg Browne (1767–1827), see Kinsky-Halm, p. 22.

11. Wegeler-Ries, pp. 50f.

12. In 1803 Haydn attempted another quartet, in B-flat major, but left it unfinished.

13. Letter of 1 July 1801, *Briefwechsel*, no. 67.

14. The complete early version is reprinted in the Appendix to this book from *Beethoven Werke*, Abteilung VI, Band 3, *Streichquartette I* (Munich, 1992). For a perceptive overview of the differences in the first movement, see Janet Levy, *Beethoven's Compositional Choices: The Two Versions of op. 18 no. 1, First Movement* (Philadelphia, 1982). Levy's book does not deal with the compositional process behind the original version as revealed in the sketches, or with those few sketches that unequivocally belong to the revision.

15. *AMZ* III (26 August 1801), col. 800, quoted in Kinsky-Halm, p. 43. This notice is not contained in Stefan Kunze's generally reliable collection of reviews, issued as *Ludwig van Beethoven: Die Werke im Spiegel Seiner Zeit* (Laaber, 1987).

16. In one of Beethoven's early sketches, he writes a passage for keyboard and then scribbles on it, "This passage is stolen from the Mozart Sinfonie in C [major?] where the Andante in 6/8 from the—" (breaks off; my translation); see *The "Kafka" Sketchbook*, ed. Joseph Kerman (London, 1967), vol. 2, p. 228; and *BML*, pp. 57–59.

17. Grasnick 1 Sketchbook, fol. 27v, written across the top of the page. I am indebted to Clemens Brenneis for making his transcription of this sketchbook available to me prior to publication.

18. For this reference I am indebted to Elaine Sisman and Daniel Stepner.

OPUS 18 NO. 1: THE FIRST MOVEMENT

1. I am excluding his uses of Allegro alone or with modifiers such as "assai," "molto," "con brio," or "vivace," though even if these were included the list of first movements in Allegro with triple meter would not be long.

2. This combination appears in the early Wind Sextet published later as op. 71, in the Piano Sonatas opp. 28 and 31 no. 3, the Violin Sonata op. 30 no. 1, and, very late in his career, in the first movement of the E-flat major quartet op. 127.

3. For a penetrating discussion of expression markings in Beethoven, see Leo Treitler, "Beethoven's 'Expressive' Markings," *BF* 7 (1999): 89–112.

4. See *Beethoven: Ein Skizzenbuch zu Streichquartetten aus Op. 18,* ed. Wilhelm Virneisel (Bonn, 1974), transcription volume, pp. 46–47 (= pp. 8–9 of the sketchbook Grasnick 2). The evocation of Juliet suggests a possible link to Giulietta Guicciardi, with whom Beethoven was in love in 1801–1802, perhaps as early as 1800, and to whom he dedicated the "Moonlight" Sonata, op. 27 no. 2.

5. Reported by Thayer, TF, p. 261; and Maynard Solomon, *Beethoven,* 2nd rev. ed. (New York, 1998), p. 110.

6. See my *Beethoven: Studies in the Creative Process* (Cambridge, Mass., 1992), pp. 209–217.

7. See David H. Smyth, "Beethoven's Revision of the Scherzo of the Quartet, op. 18 no. 1," *BF* I (1992), pp. 147–164. Although the second Scherzo version has the same number of measures as the first, the many changes in detail that Smyth discusses, involving virtually every measure of the movement, provide rich food for thought. Beethoven's critical revision of the movement enlivens the content in remarkable ways, including its dynamics, accent patterns, and features of counterpoint and occasional pitch content.

8. I define a "turning motif" as one in which the starting note of a linear figure first moves up, or down, then may return to the first pitch, then moves in the opposite direction and returns again to the first pitch. The motion may be stepwise, as in op. 18 no. 1, or by other intervals, as in the first theme of the *Eroica* Symphony, first movement.

9. Beethoven's change of meter from 4/4 to 3/4 in the sketches coincided

with his discovery of the true form of the opening motif, which in 4/4 would have needed three full beats on the first sustained F rather than two beats, thus losing momentum in its first measure.

10. Examples include the piano trio op. 1 no. 3; the piano sonatas op. 2 no. 1, op. 2 no. 2, op. 7, and op. 14 no. 1; and the F major cello sonata op. 5 no. 1.

11. *Ein Skizzenbuch zu Streichquartetten aus Op. 18,* edited and transcribed by Wilhelm Virneisel (Bonn, 1972 and 1974). Earlier, partial transcriptions of the sketches appeared in N II, pp. 476–93, esp. 481–86.

12. For a description of Grasnick 1 and 2, see JTW, pp. 72–88; on the importance of Beethoven's turn to sketchbooks, see Joseph Kerman, "Beethoven's Early Sketches," *Musical Quarterly* 56 (1970), reprinted in P. H. Lang, ed., *The Creative World of Beethoven* (New York, 1970), pp. 13–36.

13. A large mass of Beethoven earlier sketches, brought together as the portfolio called the "Kafka" miscellany, is available in facsimile and transcription in Joseph Kerman, ed., *Ludwig van Beethoven: Autograph Miscellany from circa 1786–1799, British Museum Additional MS 29801, ff. 39–162 (The "Kafka" Sketchbook),* 2 vols. (London, 1970).

14. Donald Greenfield, *Sketch Studies for Three Movements of Beethoven's String Quartets, op. 18 Nos. 1 and 2* (diss., Princeton University, 1982).

15. Eight of these were published by Nottebohm and have been accepted ever since as the earliest variant ideas for the main theme, but Greenfield shows that "at least three of Nottebohm's eight examples have nothing to do with the evolution of the 'main theme'" (Greenfield, *Sketch Studies,* p. 48).

16. Ibid., pp. 50–53.

17. I am following Greenfield's summary on the exposition sketches, pp. 116–118.

18. Ibid., pp. 117f.

19. On Amenda see Theodor Frimmel, *Beethoven-Handbuch* (Leipzig, 1926),

pp. 10f; Peter Clive, *Beethoven and His World: A Biographical Dictionary* (Oxford, 2001), pp. 5f; and Theodore Albrecht, *Letters to Beethoven* (Lincoln, Neb., 1996), I, no. 31.

20. For the text of the dedication, see Kinsky-Halm, p. 43, and *Briefwechsel,* no. 42; for the subsequent letters to Amenda, nos. 43, 44 (Summer 1799); 51 (Amenda to Beethoven, 1800/01); 66 (before July 1801); 67 (1 July [1801]). In March 1815 Amenda wrote to Beethoven again (no. 791), as warmly as before.

21. *Briefwechsel* no. 67; Anderson, no. 53.

22. The first published installment of the op. 18 quartets, with nos. 1–3, came out in June 1801 (issued by T. Mollo in Vienna); it was followed in October 1801 by the three remaining quartets. As was customary at the time, they were published only in parts, not score.

23. Carl Waack, "Beethovens F-Dur Streichquartett Op. 18 Nr. 1 in seiner ursprünglichen Fassung," *Die Musik* 3, no. 12 (1904): 418–420; Hans Josef Wedig, "Beethoven's Streichquartett op. 18 Nr. 1 und seine erste Fassung," *Veröffentlichungen des Beethovenhauses in Bonn,* 2 (Bonn, 1922). The whole Amenda version appears in W. Hess, *Supplemente zur Gesamtausgabe,* vol. 6 (Wiesbaden, 1963), and in the *Beethoven Werke,* ser. 6, vol. 3 (*Streichquartette 1*), ed. Paul Mies (Wiesbaden, 1962).

24. The recently discovered autograph manuscript of the four-hands version was sold at auction by Sotheby's on 1 December, 2005.

25. See Janet Levy, *Beethoven's Compositional Choices: The Two Versions of Opus 18, No. 1, First Movement* (Philadelphia, 1982). These remarks are based in part on my liner notes for the Pro Arte Quartet recording on Laurel Records (LR-116, 1981); and also on an unpublished paper on the movement written many years ago by George Edwards, Professor of Music at Columbia University.

26. Unless otherwise noted, measure numbers in this discussion refer to the final version.

1. TF, p. 409. Radicati, by his own testimony, had been responsible for fingering the first edition of op. 59, published in January 1808. The story was told to Thayer by Samuel Appleby, son of the English musician Thomas Appleby.

2. See Peter Clive, *Beethoven and His World* (Oxford, 2001), p. 143.

3. See my "A Problem of Form: The 'Scherzo' of Beethoven's String Quartet in F major, Op. 59 No. 1," *BF* 2 (1993): 85. I trace the anecdote back to W. von Lenz, *Beethoven: Eine Kunst-Studie* (Hamburg, 1860), Pt. II, p. 30.

4. *Briefwechsel,* no. 194, dated 10 October 1804; however, the letter says that they cannot be supplied right away, showing that at that time Beethoven was just beginning to think about composing new quartets, probably before receiving any commission.

5. *Briefwechsel,* nos. 254 (5 July 1806) and 256 (3 September 1806).

6. This probably refers not to the date of his beginning the composition but to the date on which Beethoven began writing the autograph, a sign of his awareness of the special character of this work.

7. On the autograph of op. 59 no. 1 and what it reveals, see my *Beethoven: Studies in the Creative Process,* pp. 181–197, dealing with the first movement. On the second movement of no. 1, see "A Problem of Form," pp. 85–96; also Jonathan Del Mar's comments on this movement in *BF* 8 (2001): 165–170, and my reply, pp. 170–172. The autographs of the quartets nos. 2 and 3, long available in facsimile, have yet to be studied closely and discussed in print.

8. See Alan Tyson's description of the sketchbook in JTW, pp. 146–155; and his important article, "The 'Razumovsky' Quartets: Some Aspects of the Sources," in Tyson, ed., *Beethoven Studies,* 3 (Cambridge, 1982), pp. 107–140, where the folio structure of all three autographs is also given. Tyson describes the location of the extant sketches for the op. 59 quartets, scattered as they are, and concludes from paper and other physical evidence that they were

not derived from an integral sketchbook. Nevertheless, it seems likely that such a sketchbook, which would have contained ample sketches for the first movement of no. 1, and probably material for the other two works, is indeed lost.

9. See Theodor von Frimmel, *Beethoven-Handbuch* (Leipzig, 1926; rept. Hildesheim, 2003), II, p. 162. On Anton Schreiber, see Theodore Albrecht, "'First Name Unknown': Violist Anton Schreiber, the Schuppanzigh Quartet, and Early Performances of Beethoven's String Quartets, Op. 59," *The Beethoven Journal* 19/1 (Summer 2004): 10–18.

10. See *BML*, pp. 313 and 528 n. 3. Razumovsky's busy social life figures in the memoirs of Lulu Thurheim, *Mein Leben: Erinnerungen aus Oesterreichs grosser Welt*, vol. II (Munich, 1913–1914).

11. See the recent book by one of his descendants, Maria Razumovsky, *Die Rasumovkys: Eine Familie am Zarenhof* (Cologne, 1998). This book is largely a chronicle, based on family documents, of three prominent early members of the family: Andrei Kirillovitch's father, Kirill (1728–1803), and uncle, Aleksei (1709–71), and finally Andrei Kirillovitch himself. It is of value mainly for its account of his diplomatic and social career, offering nothing of interest on his relationship to Beethoven beyond mentioning his commission of these quartets. It does contain a color reproduction (facing p. 229) of a striking late portrait of Razumovsky made in 1835 by the portraitist Ferdinand Georg Waldmüller, the same Waldmüller who made the fine portrait of Beethoven in 1823 that is generally regarded as the most realistic done in the composer's lifetime. See Alessandra Comini, *The Changing Image of Beethoven* (New York, 1987), plate 6 and pp. 65–67.

12. WoO 158/1, a posthumously published set of Continental folksongs, was composed around 1815. On these works see Barry Cooper, *Beethoven's Folksong Settings* (Oxford, 1994), and Petra Weber-Bockholdt, *Beethovens Bearbeitungen Britischer Lieder* (Munich, 1994).

13. For the sketch of the Austrian military song, see *Ludwig van Beethoven:*

Ein Skizzenbuch aus dem Jahre 1809 (Landsberg 5), 2 vols., ed. Clemens Brenneis (Bonn, 1995), esp. vol. II, pp. 20f and p. 19 of the sketchbook.

14. See *BML,* p. 316.

15. See James Webster, "Traditional Elements in Beethoven's Middle-Period String Quartets," in R. Winter and E. Derr, eds., *Beethoven: Performers and Critics: The International Beethoven Congress, Detroit 1977* (Detroit, 1980), pp. 94–133.

16. S. Kunze, *Ludwig van Beethoven: Die Werke im Spiegel seiner Zeit* (Laaber, 1987), p. 72; my translation.

17. James Webster advances cogent arguments for this relationship in "Traditional Elements in Beethoven's Middle-Period String Quartets," pp. 103ff.

18. See *BML,* pp. 325 and p. 529 n. 28.

19. For the full listing of Beethoven's metronome markings for his first eleven quartets, from op. 18 through op. 95, see N II, pp. 519–521.

OPUS 59 NO. 1: THE FIRST MOVEMENT

1. The autograph was published in facsimile by Scolar Press (London, 1980), edited by Alan Tyson.

2. For a full discussion of Beethoven's use of repeat signs at the autograph stage, see my "Process vs. Limits: A View of the Quartet in F Major, Op. 59 no. 1," in my *Beethoven: Studies in the Creative Process* (Cambridge, Mass., 1992), pp. 198–208.

3. See my "A Problem of Form: The 'Scherzo' of Beethoven's String Quartet in F Major, Op. 59 no. 1," *Beethoven Forum* 2 (1993): 85–96.

4. Other middle-period Beethoven works using this opening gambit include (with modifications) the piano concerto no. 4, first movement, and the Allegretto slow movement of the Eighth Symphony. Prominent uses of repeated-note chordal patterns in even eighth-notes include the cello sonata op. 5 no. 1, first movement opening, and the A major cello sonata op. 69,

finale (in which a figure of eight such notes plus downbeat is actually a real motif). If we include works that open with repeated pitches in "uneven" rhythms, we could add the second movement of op. 59 no. 1 (another way in which it is a close companion to the first movement), and the string trio op. 3.

5. On this aspect of his treatment of the cello, not only in the quartet but in his cello sonatas and other keyboard chamber music, see my "Beethoven's Op. 69 Revisited: The Place of the Sonata in Beethoven's Chamber Music," in Sieghard Brandenburg, Ingeborg Maass, and Wolfgang Osthoff, eds., *Beethovens Werke für Klavier und Violoncello: Bericht über die Internationale Fachkonferenz Bonn, 18–20 Juni 1998* (Bonn, 2004), pp. 145–172.

6. A striking change in the autograph is Beethoven's moving the piano dynamic from m. 9 to m. 8 in the three lower voices. That is, he first continued the crescendo in the MT from m. 1 right to the end of the cello solo, but in revision placed the *p* on the last note of the cello theme—thus lessening the sense of arrival.

7. This sort of précis follows the segment-by-segment and even phrase-by-phrase descriptions of the Beethoven piano sonatas by Donald Francis Tovey in his *A Companion to Beethoven's Pianoforte Sonatas* (London, 1931). As old-fashioned as Tovey's approach may seem to some, his book still provides a basic approach to these works by a musician of rare perception, working with the contents of each composition as it unfolds in time and offering pithy and informative comments along the way.

8. See David Eiseman, "Half-notes Demystified in the First Movement of Beethoven's String Quartet, Op. 59 no. 1," *College Music Symposium* 24/2 (1984): 21–27.

9. For a fine exegesis of the fugato passage, see Richard Kramer, "'Das Organische der Fuge': On the Autograph of Beethoven's String Quartet in F Major, Op. 59 no. 1," in C. Wolff, ed., *The String Quartets of Haydn, Mozart, and Beethoven,* Isham Library Papers III (Cambridge, Mass., 1980), pp. 223–277, including a response by Robert Winter and discussion by other scholars.

10. On the ways in which the repeat in the autograph was intended to intensify this final arrival of MT in high register, see my "Process vs. Limits."

11. See ibid., and Malcolm Miller, "Peak Experience: High Register and Structure in the 'Razumovsky' Quartets, Op. 59," in William Kinderman, ed., *The String Quartets of Beethoven* (Urbana, Ill., 2006), pp. 60-88. Miller's article singles out high-register points in all three op. 59 quartets.

THE LATE QUARTETS

1. *Briefwechsel,* no. 1508; English translation and annotation in Theodore Albrecht, ed., *Letters to Beethoven* (Lincoln, Neb., 1996), vol. 2, no. 299.

2. Lev Ginsburg, "Ludwig van Beethoven und Nikolai Galitzin," *Beethoven Jahrbuch* IV (1959-60), p. 60.

3. Letter to Schott of 19 March 1825; Anderson 1354, *Briefwechsel,* no. 1949.

4. *Briefwechsel,* no. 2003; Anderson no. 1405. A portion of the letter was published by Heinrich Schenker, with commentary, in *Der Tonwille* 6 (1923): 49-41, and by Oswald Jonas, in English translation, in "A Lesson with Beethoven by Correspondence," *The Musical Quarterly,* 38 (1952): 215-221. Most recently Schenker's discussion was translated, with up-to-date commentary, by William Drabkin in *Der Tonwille . . .* vol. II: Issues 6-10 (1923-1924) (Oxford, 2005), pp. 69-71.

5. Anderson no. 1405; translation modified.

6. See my "Beethoven's Emergence from Crisis: The Cello Sonatas of Op. 102 (1815)," *Journal of Musicology* XVI/3 (1998): 301-323.

7. For the *Tagebuch,* original text, translation, and commentary, see Maynard Solomon, "Beethoven's Tagebuch of 1812-1818," *Beethoven Studies* 3 (Cambridge, England, 1982): 193-288; also Solomon, *Beethoven Essays* (Cambridge, Mass., 1988), pp. 233-295.

8. *Ludwig van Beethoven, Konversationshefte*, 11 vols., ed. Karl-Heinz Köhler and Grita Herre (Wiesbaden, 1972–2001).

9. *Konversationshefte* of February 1820; vol. 1, p. 235.

10. For a valuable account of Beethoven's relationship to Enlightenment ideals and to the Romanticism that became a main current in his early lifetime, see Solomon, *Late Beethoven* (Berkeley, 2003), especially chapters 2, 3, and 5.

11. Holz reported this conversation years later in a letter of 1857 to Wilhelm von Lenz, who included it in his *Beethoven: Eine Kunst-Studie*, IV (1860), pp. 216f. See *BML*, pp. 441f.

12. From the anonymous review of the first performance, in *AMZ*, 1826, col. 310. See *BML*, p. 460. The anecdote reporting Beethoven's angry reponse to the reception of the fugue at op. 130's first performance has not been traced back beyond Ivan Mahaim's *Beethoven: Naissance et Renaissance des derniers quatuors* (Paris, 1964), p. 419. Maynard Solomon (in *Beethoven*, p. 485, n. 124) remarks that it may be apocryphal, but in private conversation has suggested to me that Mahaim may have derived it from a currently unknown manuscript source.

OPUS 130: THE FIRST MOVEMENT

1. The De Roda sketchbook has been preserved since 1962 in the Beethoven-Haus in Bonn as MS NE 47. The Moscow sketchbook has been published in facsimile and transcription by E. Vyaskova, *Ludwig van Beethoven, Moscow Sketchbook from 1825* (Moscow, 1995). On the origins and format of these two sketchbooks, see JTW, pp. 306–312 (De Roda) and 419–323 (Moscow).

2. Klaus Kropfinger, "Streichquartett B-Dur op. 130" in A. Riethmüller et al., eds., *Beethoven: Interpretationen seiner Werke* (Laaber, 1994), II, pp. 299–316; see also Barry Cooper, *Beethoven and the Creative Process* (Oxford, 1990), pp. 197–214.

3. De Roda, fol. 6r. Kropfinger suggests a date of May 1825 for this entry, following Sieghard Brandenburg's suggestions on the chronology of entries in the sketchbook.

4. De Roda, fol. 13v; see Kropfinger, p. 304.

5. This way of opening has some distant antecedents but none as ambiguous as this. The C minor string trio op. 9 no. 3, a remarkable early work, opens with a somewhat similar descent; in his middle period, a descending scale from 5 opens the *Leonore* Overture no. 3.

6. Pointed out in Stefania de Kennesey, "The Quartet, the Finale and the Fugue: A Study of Beethoven's op. 130/133 . . ." (diss., Princeton University, 1984; University Microfilms No. 8405149), pp. 19f.

7. The rising chromatic motion in the violin 2 at m. 8, leading to its repeat of the cello motif from m. 7, encapsulates chromatically in one measure the rising motion from B (now beginning up one step, at B-natural) to F that we saw from m. 4 to 7 in diatonic form. And the rising fourth in violin 1 at m. 11 anticipates the rising fourth figure in the oncoming Allegro (mm. 15–16).

8. Some parallels can be found as well in the second movement of the G major quartet op. 18 no. 2, and, looking further back, in the finale of Haydn's C major quartet op. 54 no. 2, with its long Adagio sections surrounding a short Presto middle section, and with its pathbreaking use of slow arpeggiated motives in the cello, ascending through more than three octaves.

9. See Joseph Kerman, "Notes on Beethoven's Codas," *Beethoven Studies 3,* ed. Alan Tyson (Cambridge, England, 1982), pp. 141–160, for a comparison of similar effects in op. 59 no. 3, first movement, and the violin sonata in G major op. 96. See also David Brodbeck and John Platoff, "Dissociation and Integration: The First Movement of Beethoven's op. 130," *19th-Century Music 7/2* (Fall 1983): 149–162.

ACKNOWLEDGMENTS

This book was originally commissioned by Margaretta Fulton of the Harvard University Press, who saw it through its early stages until her retirement in December 2005. Thereafter its editor has been Jennifer Snodgrass, who not only edited the texts with great care but videotaped the conversation sessions and took an active role in all phases of the book's preparation. We are grateful for her exemplary work. Matthew Cron prepared the annotated scores and other music examples and transcribed the conversations with care and diligence. Our thanks also go to Adam Abeshouse, who produced the recording that accompanies this book, and to the Classical Recording Foundation, which helped support it.

INDEX

Beethoven, Ludwig van *(continued)*
op. 84 *Egmont,* 219; op. 86 Mass in C Major, 22; op. 95 quartets, 3, 5, 218–219; op. 98 *An die ferne Geliebte,* 185; op. 102 cello sonata, 185; op. 103 wind octet, 36; op. 120 *Diabelli* variations, 186; op. 123 *Missa Solemnis,* 184, 186; op. 124 *Consecration of the House* overture, 184; op. 127 quartet, 184, 188, 189; op. 131 quartet, 186–189; op. 132 quartet, 14, 184, 188–190, 218, 223-224; quartet cycle, 229–230; quintet, unfinished C major, 184. *See also* Grosse Fuge op. 133; Piano sonatas (Beethoven); Quartet op. 18 no. 1; Quartet op. 59 no. 1; Quartet op. 130; Quartets op. 18; Quartets op. 59; Symphonies (Beethoven)

Berlioz, Hector, 219

Boris Godunov (Mussorgsky), 98

Boston Symphony Orchestra, 222-223

Brahms, Johannes, 122, 133

Budapest Quartet, 222

Calvino, Italo, vii

Clement, Franz, 7

Collin, Heinrich von, 100

Czerny, Carl, 68

Debussy, Claude, string quartet op. 10, 225

Don Giovanni (Mozart), 219

Dvorak, Antonin, 50

Eroica symphony. *See* Symphonies (Beethoven)

Folk melodies, 97–98

Förster, Emanuel, 12

Galitzin, Nikolai, 183–185; commission of op. 130, 193–194

"Glory Be to God in Heaven," 98

"God Save the King," 99

Greenfield, Donald, 31, 35

Grosse Fuge op. 133 (Beethoven), 37, 184, 188–189, 192, 208–209, 213, 222

Gyrowetz, Adalbert, 95

"Hammerklavier" sonata op. 106 (Beethoven), 185–186, 190, 228

"Harp" quartet op. 74 (Beethoven), 144

Haydn, Joseph, 5, 7–8, 24, 135; *The Creation,* 12; folk song settings, 98–99; "London" symphonies, 9; *The Seasons,* 12

Haydn, Joseph, quartets: op. 20, 8, 12, 14–15, 118; op. 33 no. 1, 14; op. 33 no. 3, 106; op. 55, no. 2, 14; op. 59 no. 2, 14; op. 64, 9; op. 71, 9; op. 74, 9, 14; op. 76, 9, 14, 20, 99; op. 77, 9, 12

Heiligenstadt Testament (Beethoven), 7, 20–21, 221

124–125; form and feeling, 106–
115; fugato, 112, 121, 137–138;
harmonic ambiguity, 118–120,
128–132; harmonic rhythm,
119–120; harmonies, 107, 110,
111–112, 139; main theme, 109,
123–124, 140–142; modernity of,
128, 130–132, 139, 146; opening,
106–108, 121–122; ostinato
form, 119, 121; plan of, 105–106;
recapitulation, 112–115, 126,
134–137; register, 107–108, 110,
112–113, 115–117, 136–137; repeats, 105, 119, 135; Russian
melodies, 97–98, 106, 107;
tempo, 119, 133–135, 137

Quartet op. 130 (Beethoven), 23, 59,
190–191; Alla danza tedesca,
191–192; Allegro finale, 192; Andante con moto, 191, 192; Cavatina, 23, 190, 191; finale, new,
184, 192; Grosse Fuge, 184, 188–
189, 192, 209, 213, 222; history
of, 191–192; Scherzo, 191

Quartet op. 130, first movement
(Beethoven), 193–203; Adagio,
195; Allegro opening, 194, 195;
annotated score, 232–253; character, 208, 212–213; coda, 201–
203, 206, 213, 227; conversation,
204–230; development, 199–200,
206; dynamics, 195–196; exposition, 197–199; finale, 217–218,
227–228; form of, 197–203; harmonic scheme, 194–196, 201,
207; introduction, 197–199,
204–206; key signature changes,
208–211; Moscow sketchbook,
202–203, 211–212; phrasing,
196–197; precompositional material, 193–196; recapitulation,
200–201, 211; second theme,
215–216; tempi, 197–198, 204–
205, 214–215

Quartet op. 131 (Beethoven), 184,
221, 225

Quartet op. 135 (Beethoven), 101,
184, 188–189, 219, 230; "Muss
es sein?" motto, 101, 190, 220;
sketches, 186–187

Quartets, early, 12–21. *See also* Quartets op. 18; Quartet op. 18 no.
1; Quartet op. 18 no. 1, first
movement

Quartets, late, 183–188; crossing of
genres, 190; endings, 217–218;
formal innovation in, 188–189;
fugue and variation, 189–190;
intervallic relationships 188; reception history, 221–222; slow
movements, 189–190, 192, 217;
titles and mottos, 190; voice-
leading, 190–191. *See also* Quartet op. 130; Quartet op. 130,
first movement

Quartets, middle-period, 124–125.
See also Quartets op. 59; Quartet
op. 59 no. 1

INDEX

❖